NATIONAL GEOGRAPHIC

KIDS™

NATIONAL PARKS GUIDE U.S.A.

Sarah Wassner Flynn

NATIONAL
GEOGRAPHIC

WASHINGTON, D.C.

Contents

Hawaii Volcanoes
National Park, HI

Acadia
National Park, M

Our Amazing National Parks

The world is changing at a lightning-quick pace. The population is rising, cities are growing, and new neighborhoods are popping up every single day. But amidst this changing landscape you can still find vast parcels of protected land, many of which remain virtually untouched since the days our country's settlers first arrived. These are our national parks, originally established as a way to protect the land and wildlife contained within a total of 84 million acres of stunning scenery and natural wonders.

President Theodore Roosevelt is credited with championing the establishment of the parks. A concerned environmentalist, he made it his mission to rescue these scenic spots from potential destruction by land-hungry humans. In 1872, Yellowstone, which spans Wyoming, Montana, and Idaho, became the first national park to be officially recognized by Congress. Today, there are almost 60 national parks as well as dozens of nationally protected refuges, monuments, and forests located in 49 states, plus the District of Columbia, American Samoa, Guam, Puerto Rico, Saipan, and the U.S. Virgin Islands.

This book will take you on an adventure through many of these national parks. You'll explore the exciting experiences each park has to offer, from hang gliding off a sand dune to shooting the rapids of a raging river. Maybe you'll have a chance to visit a few—or even all—of the national parks some day. In the meantime, let this book take you on an awesome cross-country journey from park to park … to park.

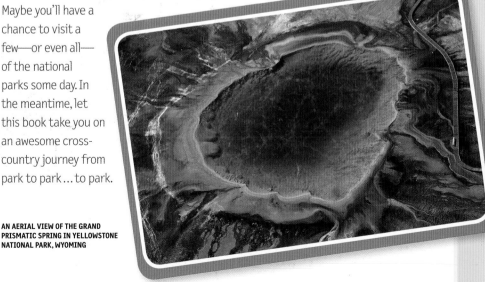

AN AERIAL VIEW OF THE GRAND PRISMATIC SPRING IN YELLOWSTONE NATIONAL PARK, WYOMING

Carlsbad Caverns National Park, NM

Everglades National Park, FL

As you journey through the parks in this guide, see if you can spot Buddy Bison! Buddy is the mascot of the National Park Trust, an organization dedicated to inspiring kids to connect with nature and our amazing parklands. For more on Buddy, visit www.buddybison.org. See page 160 for answer.

How to Use This Book!

TWENTY-FOUR PARKS ARE INTRODUCED WITH FOUR PAGES OF INFORMATION, PHOTOS, AND A MAP.

Kids: Be sure to get parent or guardian permission before trying any of the activities mentioned in this book.

3 RANGER TIPS WILL GIVE YOU IMPORTANT INFORMATION TO HELP YOU PREPARE FOR YOUR VISIT.

4 FOR GREAT WAYS TO EXPLORE THE PARK, CHECK OUT THE ACTIVITIES ON THE "DISCOVER" PAGE.

1 THE NAME OF EACH PARK CAN BE FOUND IN THE "WELCOME TO" HEADING ON ITS OPENING PAGE.

5 THE COLORED TAB ON THE RIGHT SIDE OF THE PAGE HELPS TO IDENTIFY THE REGION YOU'RE IN.

2 FOR BASIC FACTS ABOUT EACH PARK, CONSULT THE FACT BOX.

6 FOR EVEN MORE EXCITING THINGS TO ENJOY, BROWSE THE LIST OF THE FIVE MUST-DO ACTIVITIES IN EACH PARK.

7 FOR COOL AND EXCITING EXCURSIONS NEAR EACH NATIONAL PARK, CHECK OUT THE "DARE TO EXPLORE" SECTION.

8 FOR THE LOCATION OF VISITOR CENTERS AND OTHER PARK ATTRACTIONS, PERUSE THE PARK MAP. THE MINI LOCATOR MAP TELLS YOU WHAT STATE OR STATES THE PARK IS IN.

9 TO MAKE SURE YOU DON'T MISS ANYTHING FUN, KEEP TRACK OF YOUR ACTIVITIES WITH THE CHECKLIST FOUND HERE.

10 FOR A FUN AND UNIQUE BIT OF INFORMATION ABOUT EACH PARK, GO TO THE FUN FACT FOUND HERE.

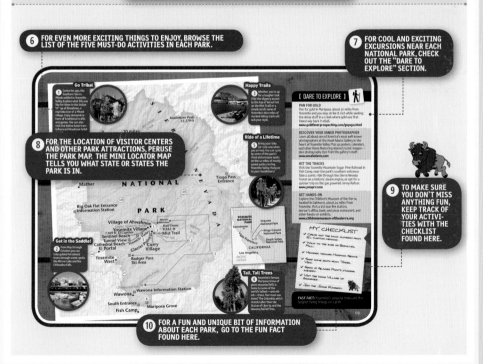

OTHER MUST-SEE NATIONAL PARK PROPERTIES IN EACH REGION ARE INTRODUCED AT THE END OF THAT SECTION.

2 THE NAMES OF PARK PROPERTIES APPEAR IN GREEN BOXES.

1 THE TITLE OF THIS SECTION IS FOUND IN THE UPPER LEFT-HAND CORNER OF THE PAGE.

3 FOR MORE INFORMATION ON ANY OF THE PARK PROPERTIES, GO TO THEIR WEBSITE. THE WEBSITE FOR EACH AREA CAN BE FOUND UNDER THE PROPERTY'S NAME.

4 THE LOCATION OF EACH PROPERTY IS FOUND NEXT TO ITS NAME. TO LOOK UP A STATE ABBREVIATION, LOOK ON THE LAST PAGE OF THE HOW TO USE SECTION.

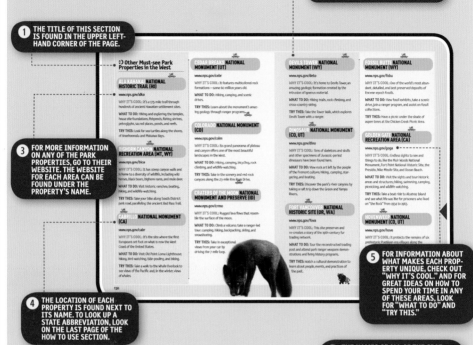

:) Other Must-see Park Properties in the West

ALA KAHAKAI NATIONAL HISTORIC TRAIL (HI)
www.nps.gov/alka

WHY IT'S COOL: It's a 175-mile trail through hundreds of ancient Hawaiian settlement sites.

WHAT TO DO: Hiking and exploring the temples, house site foundation, fishponds, fishing shrines, petroglyphs, sacred places, ponds, and reefs.

TRY THIS: Look for sea turtles along the shores of Anaehoomalu and Makalawa Bays.

BIGHORN CANYON NATIONAL RECREATION AREA (MT, WY)
www.nps.gov/bica

WHY IT'S COOL: It has steep canyon walls and is home to a diversity of wildlife, including wild horses, black bears, bighorn rams, and mule deer.

WHAT TO DO: Visit historic ranches; boating, hiking, and wildlife-watching.

TRY THIS: Take your bike along South District park road, paralleling the ancient Bad Pass Trail.

CABRILLO NATIONAL MONUMENT (CA)
www.nps.gov/cabr

WHY IT'S COOL: It's the site where the first Europeans set foot on what is now the West Coast of the United States.

WHAT TO DO: Visit Old Point Loma Lighthouse; hiking, bird-watching, tide-pooling, and biking.

TRY THIS: Take a walk to the Whale Overlook to see views of the Pacific and, in the winter, views of whales.

CEDAR BREAKS NATIONAL MONUMENT (UT)
www.nps.gov/cebr

WHY IT'S COOL: It features multicolored rock formations—some 60 million years old.

WHAT TO DO: Hiking, camping, and scenic drives.

TRY THIS: Learn about the monument's amazing geology through ranger programs.

COLORADO NATIONAL MONUMENT (CO)
www.nps.gov/colm

WHY IT'S COOL: Its grand panorama of plateau and canyon offers one of the most beautiful landscapes in the West.

WHAT TO DO: Hiking, camping, bicycling, rock climbing, and wildlife-watching.

TRY THIS: Take in the scenery and red-rock canyons along the 23-mile Rim Rock Drive.

CRATERS OF THE MOON NATIONAL MONUMENT AND PRESERVE (ID)
www.nps.gov/crmo

WHY IT'S COOL: Rugged lava flows that resemble the surface of the moon.

WHAT TO DO: Climb a volcano; take a ranger-led tour; camping, hiking, backpacking, skiing, and snowshoeing.

TRY THIS: Take in exceptional views from your car by driving the 7-mile loop.

DEVILS TOWER NATIONAL MONUMENT (WY)
www.nps.gov/deto

WHY IT'S COOL: It's home to Devils Tower, an amazing geologic formation created by the intrusion of igneous material.

WHAT TO DO: Hiking, trails, rock climbing, and cross-country skiing.

TRY THIS: Take the Tower Walk, which explores Devils Tower with a ranger.

DINOSAUR NATIONAL MONUMENT (CO, UT)
www.nps.gov/dino

WHY IT'S COOL: Tons of skeletons and skulls and other specimens of Jurassic-period dinosaurs have been found here.

WHAT TO DO: View rock art left by the people of the Fremont culture; hiking, camping, star-gazing, and boating.

TRY THIS: Discover the park's river canyons by taking a raft trip down the Green and Yampa Rivers.

FORT VANCOUVER NATIONAL HISTORIC SITE (OR, WA)
www.nps.gov/fova

WHY IT'S COOL: This site preserves and re-creates a story of the 19th-century fur trading network.

WHAT TO DO: Tour the reconstructed trading post and other cultural and living history programs.

TRY THIS: Watch a cultural demonstration to learn about people, events, and practices of the past.

FOSSIL BUTTE NATIONAL MONUMENT (WY)
www.nps.gov/fobu

WHY IT'S COOL: One of the world's most abundant, detailed, and best preserved deposits of Eocene-epoch fossils.

WHAT TO DO: View fossil exhibits, take a scenic drive, join a ranger program, and assist on fossil collections.

TRY THIS: Have a picnic under the shade of aspen trees at the Chicken Creek Picnic Area.

GOLDEN GATE NATIONAL RECREATION AREA (CA)
www.nps.gov/goga

WHY IT'S COOL: Endless sights to see and things to do, like the Muir Woods National Monument, Fort Point National Historic Site, the Presidio, Nike Missile Site, and Ocean Beach.

WHAT TO DO: Visit the sights and tour historic areas and structures; hiking, swimming, camping, picnicking, and wildlife-watching.

TRY THIS: Take a boat ride to Alcatraz Island and see what life was like for prisoners who lived on "the Rock" from 1934 to 1963.

HOVENWEEP NATIONAL MONUMENT (CO, UT)
www.nps.gov/hove

WHY IT'S COOL: It protects the remains of six prehistoric Puebloan-era villages along the...

5 FOR INFORMATION ABOUT WHAT MAKES EACH PROPERTY UNIQUE, CHECK OUT "WHY IT'S COOL." AND FOR GREAT IDEAS ON HOW TO SPEND YOUR TIME IN ANY OF THESE AREAS, LOOK FOR "WHAT TO DO" AND "TRY THIS."

FOLLOWING THE FEATURED PARKS IS A SECTION ON SPOTLIGHTED PARKS— MORE INCREDIBLE DESTINATIONS TO ADD TO YOUR TRAVEL LIST.

7 THE NAMES OF ALL OF THE SPOTLIGHTED PARKS APPEAR IN GREEN BOXES. FOR PARK WEBSITES, GO TO THE "FIND OUT MORE" SECTION AT THE END OF THIS BOOK.

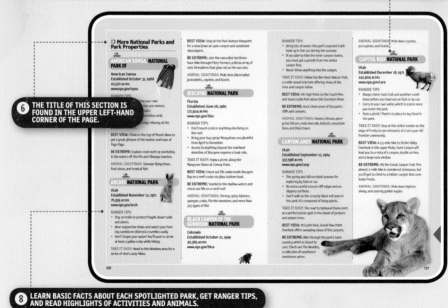

:) More National Parks and Park Properties

AMERICAN SAMOA NATIONAL PARK OF
American Samoa
Established October 31, 1988
10,520 acres
www.nps.gov/npsa

RANGER TIPS
...are remote...
Page Pago...
...a day relaxing at the...

BEST VIEW: Climb to the top of Mount Alava to get a great glimpse of the harbor and town of Page Pago.

BE EXTREME: Explore coral reefs by snorkeling in the waters of the Ofu and Olosega beaches.

ANIMAL SIGHTINGS: Samoan flying foxes, fruit doves, and tropical fish.

6 THE TITLE OF THIS SECTION IS FOUND IN THE UPPER LEFT-HAND CORNER OF THE PAGE.

ARCHES NATIONAL PARK
Utah
Established November 12, 1971
76,359 acres
www.nps.gov/arch

RANGER TIPS
• Stay on trails to protect fragile desert soils and plants.
• Wear supportive shoes and watch your footing; sandstone slickrock crumbles easily.
• Don't forget your water! You'll want to drink at least a gallon a day while hiking.

TAKE IT EASY: Head to the Windows area for a series of short, easy hikes.

BEST VIEW: Stop at the Park Avenue Viewpoint for a view down an open canyon and sandstone skyscrapers.

BE EXTREME: Join the naturalist-led three-hour hike through Fiery Furnace, a dense array of rock formations that glow red as the sun sets.

ANIMAL SIGHTINGS: Mule deer, black-tailed jackrabbits, coyotes, and lizards.

BISCAYNE NATIONAL PARK
Florida
Established June 28, 1980
172,924 acres
www.nps.gov/bisc

RANGER TIPS
• Don't touch coral or anything else living on the reef.
• Bring your bug spray! Mosquitoes are plentiful from April to December.
• Access to anything beyond the mainland shoreline of Biscayne requires a boat ride.

TAKE IT EASY: Enjoy a picnic along the Mangrove Shore at Convoy Point.

BEST VIEW: Check out life underneath Biscayne Bay on a reef cruise via glass-bottom boat.

BE EXTREME: Snorkel in the shallow waters and check out life on a coral reef.

ANIMAL SIGHTINGS: Shrimp, spiny lobsters, sponges, crabs, Florida manatees, and more than 325 types of fish.

BLACK CANYON OF THE GUNNISON NATIONAL PARK
Colorado
Established October 21, 1999
30,385 acres
www.nps.gov/blca

RANGER TIPS
• Bring lots of water; the park's exposed trails heat up in the sun during the summer.
• If you plan to take the inner canyon routes, you must get a permit from the visitor center first.
• Never throw anything into the canyon.

TAKE IT EASY: Follow the Rim Rock Nature Trail, a 1-mile round-trip trek offering views of the river and canyon below.

BEST VIEW: Hit High Point on the South Rim and stand 2,689 feet above the Gunnison River.

BE EXTREME: Rock climb some of the park's cliffs and canyons.

ANIMAL SIGHTINGS: Ravens, falcons, peregrine falcons, mule deer, elk, bobcats, mountain lions, and black bears

CANYONLANDS NATIONAL PARK
Utah
Established September 12, 1964
337,598 acres
www.nps.gov/cany

RANGER TIPS
• The spring and fall are ideal seasons for exploring by foot or car.
• Be extra careful around cliff edges and on slippery surfaces.
• Don't walk on the crunchy black soil seen in the park; it's composed of living plants.

TAKE IT EASY: The road to Upheaval Dome ends at a perfect picnic spot in the shade of junipers and pinyon trees.

BEST VIEW: At 6,080 feet, Grand View Point Overlook offers sweeping views of the canyons.

BE EXTREME: Bike through the park's backcountry, which is closed to cars. Check out The Needles, a collection of weathered sandstone spires.

ANIMAL SIGHTINGS: Mule deer, coyotes, porcupines, and lizards

CAPITOL REEF NATIONAL PARK
Utah
Established December 18, 1971
241,904 acres
www.nps.gov/care

RANGER TIPS
• Always check road, trail, and weather conditions before you head out on foot or by car.
• Carry in your own water, which is scarce once you enter the park.
• Pack a picnic! There's no place to buy food in the park.

TAKE IT EASY: Stop at the visitor center on the edge of Fruita to see remnants of a 120-year-old frontier community.

BEST VIEW: A 2.5-mile hike to Strike Valley Overlook in the upper Muley Twist Canyon will lead you to a vista of canyons, double arches, and a large rock window.

BE EXTREME: Hit the Cohab Canyon Trail. This almost 2-mile hike is considered strenuous, but it's great to climb to a hidden canyon that overlooks Fruita.

ANIMAL SIGHTINGS: Mule deer, bighorn sheep, and soaring golden eagles

8 LEARN BASIC FACTS ABOUT EACH SPOTLIGHTED PARK, GET RANGER TIPS, AND READ HIGHLIGHTS OF ACTIVITIES AND ANIMALS.

NATIONAL PARK MAP KEY

1	Bulleted feature	)=====(	Tunnel
▦	Point of interest	•••••	Trail
•	City	┼──┼	Railroad/Tram
▲	Campground	•••••	Ferry/Canoe route
△	Elevation	─────	River
↑N	North arrow	─ ─ ─	Intermittent river
〰	Overpass	▨	National Park (N.P.) National Park and Preserve National Preserve National Memorial Parkway
⊐⊢	Dam	▨	National Grassland
⅄	Falls	▨	National Forest
○	Spring	▨	National Monument (Nat. Mon.) National Wildlife Refuge
⑦⑦	U.S. Interstate highway	▨	Indian Reservation (U.S.) or Indian Reserve (Canadian)
⑳	U.S. Federal highway	▨	State Park
⑫	State highway	◠	Lake
⑥	Provincial highway (Canadian)	◡	Glacier
22	Other road	≈≈	Swamp
▬▬	National boundary		
─ ──	State boundary		
··········	Continental Divide		
═══	Road		

LIST OF STATE AND TERRITORY ABBREVIATIONS

Alabama: AL
Alaska: AK
American Samoa: AS
Arizona: AZ
Arkansas: AR
California: CA
Colorado: CO
Connecticut: CT
Delaware: DE
District of Columbia: DC
Florida: FL
Georgia: GA
Guam: GU
Hawaii: HI

Idaho: ID
Illinois: IL
Indiana: IN
Iowa: IA
Kansas: KS
Kentucky: KY
Louisiana: LA
Maine: ME
Maryland: MD
Massachusetts: MA
Michigan: MI
Minnesota: MN
Mississippi: MS
Missouri: MO

Montana: MT
Nebraska: NE
Nevada: NV
New Hampshire: NH
New Jersey: NJ
New Mexico: NM
New York: NY
North Carolina: NC
North Dakota: ND
Ohio: OH
Oklahoma: OK
Oregon: OR
Pennsylvania: PA
Puerto Rico: PR

Rhode Island: RI
South Carolina: SC
South Dakota: SD
Tennessee: TN
Texas: TX
U.S. Virgin Islands: VI
Utah: UT
Vermont: VT
Virginia: VA
Washington: WA
West Virginia: WV
Wisconsin: WI
Wyoming: WY

National Parks in the United States and Territories

North Cascades N.P.

OLYMPIC NATIONAL PARK
page 110

Washington

MOUNT RAINIER NATIONAL PARK
page 106

GLACIER NATIONAL PARK
page 86

CANADA
U.S.

Montana

THEODORE ROOSEVELT NATIONAL PARK
page 46

North Dakota

Oregon

Crater Lake N.P.

Idaho

YELLOWSTONE NATIONAL PARK
page 118

South Dakota

GRAND TETON NATIONAL PARK
page 90

Redwood N.P.

WIND CAVE NATIONAL PARK
page 50

BADLANDS NATIONAL PARK
page 38

Lassen Volcanic N.P.

Wyoming

Nevada

California

Nebraska

BRYCE CANYON NATIONAL PARK
page 78

ROCKY MOUNTAIN NATIONAL PARK
page 114

YOSEMITE NATIONAL PARK
page 122

Great Basin N.P.

Utah

Capitol Reef N.P.

Colorado

Kings Canyon N.P.

ZION NATIONAL PARK
page 126

Arches N.P.

Black Canyon of the Gunnison N.P.

Kansas

Sequoia N.P.

Canyonlands N.P.

Great Sand Dunes N.P. & Preserve

Death Valley N.P.

Mesa Verde N.P.

Channel Islands N.P.

GRAND CANYON NATIONAL PARK
page 68

JOSHUA TREE NATIONAL PARK
page 102

Petrified Forest N.P.

Oklah

Arizona

New Mexico

UNITED STATES
MEXICO

Saguaro N.P.

CARLSBAD CAVERNS NATIONAL PARK
page 64

Guadalupe Mountains N.P.

Texas

Kobuk Valley N.P.

Gates of the Arctic N.P. & Preserve

BIG BEND NATIONAL PARK
page 60

Alaska

DENALI NATIONAL PARK & PRESERVE
page 82

Lake Clark N.P. & Preserve

Wrangell-St.Elias N.P. & Preserve

Katmai N.P. & Preserve

Kenai Fjords N.P.

Glacier Bay N.P. & Preserve

0   400 miles

0   400 kilometers

0   400 miles

0   400 kilometers

MAP KEY

ACADIA NATIONAL PARK
page 16
Bold, uppercase type indicates featured park in this book.

Voyageurs N.P.

Isle Royale N.P.

Maine

CANADA

U.S.

ACADIA NATIONAL PARK
page 16

Vermont   New Hampshire

Minnesota

Wisconsin

Michigan

New York

Massachusetts

Rhode Island
Connecticut

Iowa

Pennsylvania

CUYAHOGA NATIONAL PARK
page 42

New Jersey

Illinois

Indiana

Ohio

Delaware

West Virginia

Shenandoah N.P.

Maryland

Virginia

Missouri

Kentucky

Mammoth Cave N.P.

North Carolina

GREAT SMOKY MOUNTAINS NATIONAL PARK
page 24

Tennessee

Arkansas

South Carolina

Congaree N.P.

HOT SPRINGS NATIONAL PARK
page 28

Mississippi

Alabama

Georgia

Alaska (U.S.)

U.S. Virgin Islands N.P.

Hawai'i (U.S.)

PACIFIC OCEAN

Louisiana

Florida

National Park of American Samoa

Hawai'i

EVERGLADES NATIONAL PARK
page 20

Biscayne N.P.

Dry Tortugas N.P.

HALEAKALĀ NATIONAL PARK
page 94

0   200 miles

0   200 kilometers

HAWAI'I VOLCANOES NATIONAL PARK
page 98

the East

Everglades National Park

A Florida panther treks carefully through the wet and wild landscape of the Everglades, one of the East's most unique habitats.

13

the East

IN THE 1930S, increased automobile travel and new highways made the eastern region of the country more accessible than ever. As a result, people began flocking to this area and its national parks, which eventually became some of the most popular in the country. Today, the northeast and southeast remain a magnet for national park enthusiasts. Three of this region's parks—Acadia, Great Smoky Mountains, and Shenandoah—receive millions of visitors each year.

Here, you'll pretty much see it all: thick forests, sparkling lakes, meandering streams, bubbling hot springs, and beaches rimmed by coral reefs. There are peaks towering nearly 7,000 feet in the sky and deep caves carved out almost 400 feet below the ground. There are parks set in the heart of the city, and others out in the wilderness. Rich historical sites highlight the birth and growth of our country. And wherever you roam, the diversity of the region's parks provides habitat for a wide variety of animals. Simply put, from the mountains meeting the sea in Acadia to the fields of flowers in Shenandoah, the region's biodiversity is breathtaking—and beyond vast.

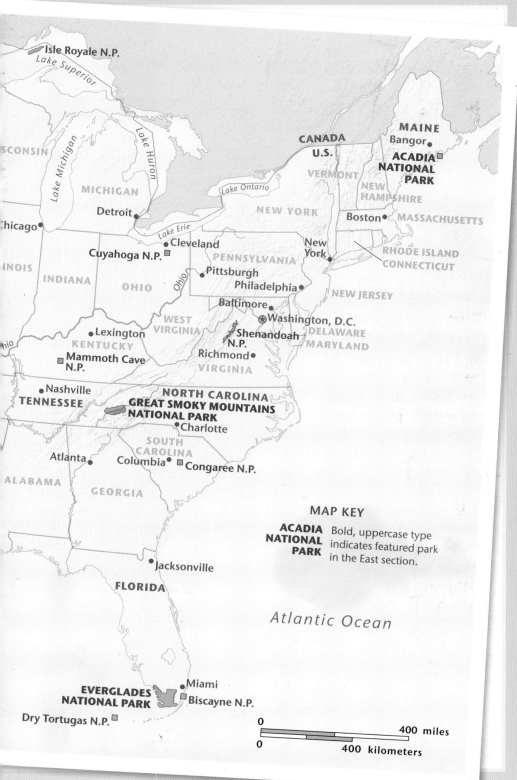

Isle Royale N.P.
Lake Superior

WISCONSIN

Lake Michigan

MICHIGAN

Lake Huron

Detroit

Chicago

Lake Erie

Cleveland

Cuyahoga N.P.

ILLINOIS

INDIANA

OHIO

Ohio

PENNSYLVANIA

Pittsburgh

Philadelphia

Baltimore

WEST
VIRGINIA

Washington, D.C.

Shenandoah
N.P.

DELAWARE

MARYLAND

Lexington

KENTUCKY

Richmond

VIRGINIA

Ohio

Mammoth Cave
N.P.

Nashville

TENNESSEE

NORTH CAROLINA
GREAT SMOKY MOUNTAINS
NATIONAL PARK

Charlotte

Atlanta

Columbia

SOUTH
CAROLINA

Congaree N.P.

ALABAMA

GEORGIA

CANADA
U.S.

VERMONT

NEW YORK

Lake Ontario

MAINE

Bangor

ACADIA
NATIONAL
PARK

NEW
HAMPSHIRE

Boston

MASSACHUSETTS

New
York

RHODE ISLAND

CONNECTICUT

NEW JERSEY

MAP KEY

ACADIA
NATIONAL
PARK

Bold, uppercase type
indicates featured park
in the East section.

Jacksonville

FLORIDA

Atlantic Ocean

EVERGLADES
NATIONAL PARK

Miami

Biscayne N.P.

Dry Tortugas N.P.

0   400 miles

0   400 kilometers

15

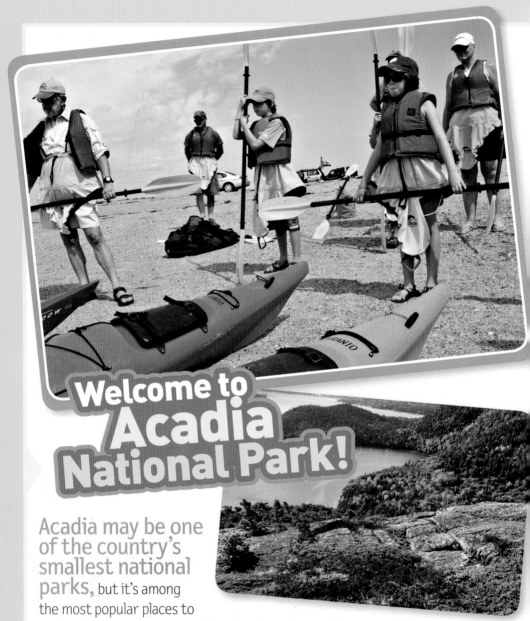

Welcome to Acadia National Park!

Acadia may be one of the country's smallest national parks, but it's among the most popular places to visit, with more than two million people exploring this scenic spot in southern Maine each year. The park occupies two-thirds of Mount Desert Island as well as a collection of smaller islands and a portion of mainland Maine. In Acadia, you'll see glacial lakes, granite cliffs dropping into the ocean, sandy beaches, and dense forests. Hit some of the 120-plus miles of hiking trails here and you'll be granted access to an up-close-and-personal tour of one of the most beautiful places in the world.

State: Maine
Established: February 26, 1919
Size: 47,748 acres
Website: www.nps.gov/acad

DISCOVER ACADIA

BEST VIEWS

Head to Schoodic Peninsula's 6-mile one-way loop, which offers great views of cool lighthouses, soaring seabirds, and forest-covered islands. It's also a great place to take a bike ride or go for a hike! Acadia Mountain (below) also offers stunning views of the park.

RANGER TIPS

Weather in Acadia changes often, so wear layers to be ready for any temperature. And if your trail goes along the ocean, make sure you know the tide schedule—during high tide, some pathways become covered in cold water.

TAKE IT EASY

Find a spot at Sand Beach, nestled along the rocky shores of Mount Desert Island (top). Fly a kite with the help of the cool breeze blowing off the ocean, sink your feet into the crushed-shell sand, or brave a splash in the 55-degree surf. For warmer waters, head to Echo Lake Beach.

BE EXTREME

Want to scale new heights? Climbers of all ages and abilities can take a rock-climbing class (center) at Acadia Mountain Guides and "learn the ropes" of scaling Acadia's pink-granite cliffs. Love the water? Try kayaking around Mount Desert Island.

ALL ABOUT ANIMALS

Stand along the shore of Mount Desert Island and you'll likely see one of the 270 species of birds that call Acadia home, including bald eagles and peregrine falcons. You may also spot harbor seals, white-tailed deer (below), red foxes, beavers, black bears, and even a breaching humpback whale out in the ocean.

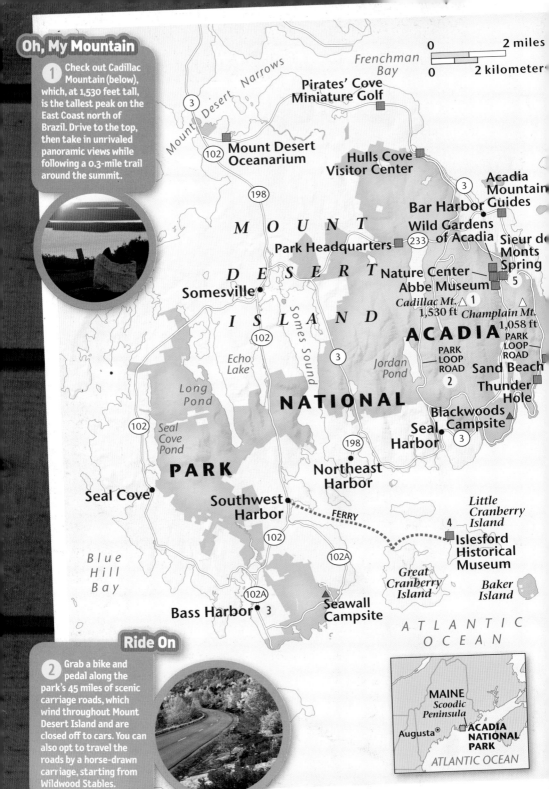

Oh, My Mountain

1 Check out Cadillac Mountain (below), which, at 1,530 feet tall, is the tallest peak on the East Coast north of Brazil. Drive to the top, then take in unrivaled panoramic views while following a 0.3-mile trail around the summit.

Ride On

2 Grab a bike and pedal along the park's 45 miles of scenic carriage roads, which wind throughout Mount Desert Island and are closed off to cars. You can also opt to travel the roads by a horse-drawn carriage, starting from Wildwood Stables.

0   2 miles
0   2 kilometer

Frenchman Bay

Mount Desert Narrows

Pirates' Cove Miniature Golf

3

102

Mount Desert Oceanarium

Hulls Cove Visitor Center

198

3

Acadia Mountain Guides

Bar Harbor

M O U N T

Wild Gardens of Acadia

233

Sieur de Monts Spring

Park Headquarters

Nature Center

Abbe Museum

D E S E R T

5

Somesville

Cadillac Mt. △ 1
1,530 ft   △
Champlain Mt.
1,058 ft

I S L A N D

102

Somes Sound

A C A D I A

PARK LOOP ROAD

Echo Lake

3

Jordan Pond

PARK LOOP ROAD

2

PARK LOOP ROAD

Sand Beach

Long Pond

N A T I O N A L

Thunder Hole

102

Seal Cove Pond

Blackwoods Campsite

Seal Harbor

3

P A R K

198

Seal Cove

Northeast Harbor

Little Cranberry Island

Southwest Harbor

FERRY

4

Islesford Historical Museum

102

102A

Blue Hill Bay

Great Cranberry Island

Baker Island

102A

Bass Harbor   3

Seawall Campsite

A T L A N T I C O C E A N

MAINE
Scoodic Peninsula

Augusta

ACADIA NATIONAL PARK

ATLANTIC OCEAN

18

Light It Up

3 Explore the grounds of the Bass Harbor Lighthouse (left) on Mount Desert Island. Built in 1858, the lighthouse is still fully functional, warning approaching boats of the Bass Harbor Bar, a large sandbar connecting downtown Bar Harbor to Bar Island.

Cruise By

4 From mid-May to October, take the ranger-led Islesford Historical Cruise. You'll make a 45-minute stop at Little Cranberry Island's Ilesford Historical Museum for a trip back in time to the tiny island's maritime past.

Straight to the Heart

5 The Sieur de Monts Spring (translation: "heart of the park") is the site of the Nature Center and the Abbe Museum (left), where you can learn about the culture and traditions of Maine Native Americans. It's also the site of the Wild Gardens of Acadia and the start of many hikes throughout the park.

[DARE TO EXPLORE]

ALL ABOUT THE OCEAN
Get hands-on with the aquatic animals of the area at the Mount Desert Oceanarium in Bar Harbor, one of the few remaining lobster hatcheries in the world. **www.theoceanarium.com**

HOLE IN ONE
For some post-park fun, hit Pirate's Cove Miniature Golf in Bar Harbor, where you can putt around an authentic, full-size pirate ship, under waterfalls, and through caves. **www.piratescove.net**

WHALE-WATCH
During the summer, head out on the ocean on a whale-watching boat. Keep your eyes peeled for a playful humpback, which just may leap out of the water right in front of you!
www.barharborwhales.com

PICK BLUEBERRIES
From mid-July through August, blueberries are bountiful throughout Maine, including the sunnier spots in Acadia National Park. Grab a bucket and hit the trails leading up to Champlain or Cadillac Mountains, where you're sure to snag a sweet snack.

MY CHECKLIST

✔ Listen to waves crashing on the shore at Thunder Hole Rock Cavern.

✔ Drive the Park Loop.

✔ Bike, hike, or take a horse-drawn carriage tour along carriage roads.

✔ Learn about the park's plants and wildlife at an exhibit at the Nature Center.

✔ Stroll the Schoodic Peninsula.

✔ Look for creatures, like crabs and sea stars, in tidepools along the coast.

✔ Hop on a ranger-narrated boat cruise.

FAST FACT: The light in the Bass Harbor Lighthouse has not been turned off in more than 150 years.

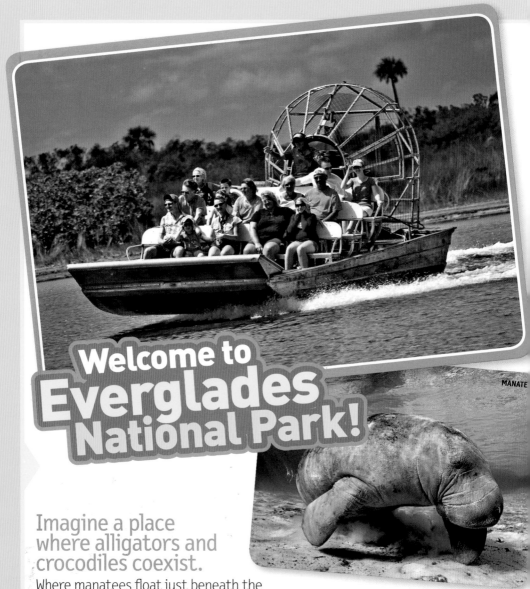

MANATE

Welcome to Everglades National Park!

Imagine a place where alligators and crocodiles coexist.

Where manatees float just beneath the surface of a slow-moving river. And where black panthers prowl the dense tropical woodlands. That's just what you'll find in Everglades National Park, a protected area of wetlands in southeast Florida. Made up of marshes, swamps, a river, and a bay, Everglades serves as host to an abundance of wildlife, from algae to alligators. It's here where more than 700 kinds of plants, 120 types of trees, and countless animals (including many on the endangered species list) grow and thrive, making Everglades one of the most ecologically diverse parks on the planet.

State: Florida
Established: December 6, 1947
Size: 1,507,850 acres
Website: www.nps.gov/ever

DISCOVER EVERGLADES

RANGER TIPS

Wear long pants, cover your arms, and spray on insect repellent to avoid mosquitoes, which are around all year long. Also leave the wildlife alone (below) and avoid collecting plants, an activity prohibited in the park. ☙

Do not feed or approach alligators: $ 5,000 FINE MAX.

TAKE IT EASY

Unwind and eat at designated picnic spots, including Paurotis Point, Nine Mile Pond, and West Lake. You can also take a half-mile walk around Flamingo Bay, a protected marine nursery.

BE EXTREME

Kayak out to the park's Ten Thousand Islands (below). You'll get unrivaled views from the water while cutting through mangroves and oyster beds. Don't be surprised if you're suddenly surrounded by feeding manatees or friendly dolphins! ☙

BEST VIEWS

Take a bike ride along Tram Road and stop at the halfway point, where you'll find a 65-foot-high observation tower (above). Climb to the top and be rewarded with an unobstructed panoramic view of the Everglades. ☙

ALL ABOUT ANIMALS

Home to a host of wildlife, the Everglades is a unique place, where you'll see dozens of endangered species in their natural habitat, including the swallowtail butterfly, American crocodile, leatherback turtle, bald eagle (below), West Indian manatee, and Florida panther. ☙

Take a Hike

3 There are four groups of trails in the 'Glades, each offering unique angles of the park's diverse ecosystem. The half-mile Anhinga Trail is your best bet for spotting wildlife, while the half-mile Mahogany Hammock Trail leads you to the largest living mahogany tree in the country.

Map Key
△ "Chickee" campsite **5**

75

41 TAMIAMI
29

Everglades City • Gulf Coast Visitor Center
29 **Chokoloskee** △

TRAIL

BIG LOOP ROAD
CYPRESS 41 TAMIAMI TRAIL

1 **Shark Valley Visitor Center**
TRAM ROAD

NATIONAL 2

W I L D E R N E S S **PRESERVE** ■ **Observation**
Tower
W A T E R W A Y
T H E

4 △
EVERGLADES

Ten Thousand Islands

△ *E V E R G L A D E S* 9336

G u l f o f
M e x i c o

△ **NATIONAL**
1 **Ernest F. Coe Visitor Center**

● Tallahassee ATLANTIC OCEAN

Orlando ●
Tampa ●
FLORIDA

Gulf of Mexico

P A R K 3

△ ■ **Mahogany Hammoc**
Paurotis Pond

EVERGLADES NATIONAL PARK
● Miami
Biscayne National Park

Dry Tortugas National Park ■

△ △ ■ **Nine Mile Pond**
West Lake

Whitewater Bay △

△ △△

0 _____ 10 miles
0 _____ 10 kilometers

C a p e   S a b l e

SNAKE BIGHT TRAIL 2
1 *Snake Bight*

△

1 ■
Flamingo Visitor Center

F l o r i d a Bay

Take a Tour

1 Make the most of your visit by signing up for one of the many ranger programs, which start at the park's various visitor centers. Spot wildlife, get a glimpse of geological formations, and pick up fascinating facts about the 'Glades as you tour by foot, canoe, tram, or airboat (right).

Go Fish

4 Hop in a canoe or kayak and cast a line into the inland and coastal waters of the Everglades and see if you can reel in fish like snapper, sea trout, bass, and tarpon. A fishing license is required within the park; check in with the visitor center for information about fishing tours and boat rentals.

Set Up Camp

5 From the beach to the woods, you can camp out throughout the park. Check out the "chickees"—elevated camping platforms—(left) available in various spots. Reservations or permits may be required depending on where you camp, so call the visitor center before your trip.

Ride On

2 Bike the 15-mile scenic loop at Shark Valley (left), an excellent way to view the 'Glades at your own pace. The trip takes two to three hours and there are no shortcuts, so make sure you're up to the task. For a less strenuous ride, bike along the Snake Bight Trail, one of the park's best bird-watching trails.

(Map labels: 27, 826, 997, Miami, 41, 1, Homestead, Royal Palm Visitor Center (Anhinga Trail), 1, ATLANTIC OCEAN)

[DARE TO EXPLORE]

PARK HOP

There are other equally amazing parks and preserves within a quick drive from Everglades. Take day trips to Biscayne National Park (20 miles east, home of the northernmost living coral reef in the continental United States and great for snorkeling and glass-bottom boat rides); Dry Tortugas National Park (check out an abandoned 19th-century brick fortress and more than 200 shipwrecks); or Big Cypress National Preserve (the H. P. Williams and Oasis Wildlife Viewing Platforms are excellent for alligator scoping).

BIG BOUNTY

Stroll the grounds of the Fruit & Spice Park in nearby Homestead, Florida, where more than 500 varieties of fruits (including 75 types of bananas alone!), vegetables, and nuts grow. Hungry? Munch on some of the park's samplings at the Mango Café. **www.fruitandspicepark.org**

STONE HOME

Check out Coral Castle—also in Homestead—a sculpture carved out of more than 1,100 tons of coral rock that took one man almost 30 years to build! Take a tour to learn how he did it and to see cool features, like functioning rocking chairs, a telescope, and a 9-ton gate that moves with just the touch of a finger—all made entirely out of stone. **www.coralcastle.com**

MY CHECKLIST

- ✔ Meet up with a park ranger for a fun guided tour by foot or by boat.
- ✔ Pedal around Shark Valley or the Snake Bight Trail.
- ✔ Paddle in a canoe or kayak to enjoy views on the water.
- ✔ Hike the 150-plus miles of nature trails the park has to offer.
- ✔ Take a two-hour, narrated tour of the Tamiami Trail on an open-air tram.
- ✔ Check out the oldest living mahogany tree in the U.S.
- ✔ Enjoy a picnic at Paurotis Point, Nine Mile Pond, or West Lake.

FAST FACT: The Everglades are home to more than one million American alligators.

Welcome to Great Smoky Mountains National Park!

Rushing waterfalls, bubbling creeks, and many, many mountains: These are just a few features of Great Smoky Mountains National Park. Straddling the Tennessee–North Carolina border, the park covers 800 square miles of rugged terrain. Most of the nine million yearly visitors see the sights by car, taking a drive on the 384 miles of mountain roads running through the park. But there's plenty to see by foot, too, thanks to the seemingly unending hiking trails that take you through the Smokies' dense forests and up the craggy peaks.

States: North Carolina and Tennessee
Established: June 15, 1934
Size: 521,590 acres
Website: www.nps.gov/grsm

DISCOVER
GREAT SMOKY MOUNTAINS

RANGER TIPS

Want to spot wildlife? Head out in the morning or evening to open areas like Cataloochee or Cades Cove.

TAKE IT EASY

Pack a picnic and seek out a shady spot at one of the many picnic areas in the park. Chimneys, a wooded area on the Tennessee side of the Smokies, has tables overlooking the West Prong of the Little Pigeon River. Or take a stroll on the many quiet trails (top).

BE EXTREME

Soar to new heights by hiking the trail to Ramsey Cascades (below), the tallest waterfall in the park. Just make sure you've got the climb in you: Eight miles long and escalating 2,000 feet in elevation, it's considered a very challenging hike.

BEST VIEWS

From April to November, head up to the observation platform (left) on top of Clingmans Dome. There's no higher point in the park—and no better view of the Smokies.

ALL ABOUT ANIMALS

There's a reason the American black bear (below) is the symbol of the Smokies: More than 1,500 of them live here (that's two bears per square mile)! This protected habitat is also home to deer, elk, 200 species of birds, and a whopping 30 species of salamanders.

2 Grab your rod and spend some time on the shores of Fontana Lake or along the banks of the 700 miles of fishable streams throughout the Smokies. Brook, rainbow, and brown trout abound; just check in with the park's visitor center to ask about a fishing license.

GREAT SMOKY MOUNTAINS NATIONAL PARK

Nashville◉ Oneida•
TENNESSEE
NORTH CAROLINA
•Raleigh
•Gainesville
Atlanta◉
GEORGIA
ATLANTIC OCEAN

0 ———— 6 miles
0 ———— 6 kilometers

FOOTHILLS PKWY.
Little River
Little Pigeon River

321
321
73
3
Gatlinburg Welcome Center
Greenbrier
Gatlinburg

NEWFOUND GAP ROAD

Sugarlands Visitor Center
Townsend Visitor Center
Elkmont
TREMONT ROAD
Chimney Tops
1
441

LAUREL CREEK ROAD

CADES COVE LOOP ROAD 3
3

Abrams Creek
1
5
CLINGMANS DOME ROAD

△ Clingmans Dome 6,643 ft

Cades Cove Visitor Center

•Chilhowee

GREAT SMOKY

MOUNTAINS

NATIONAL PARK

TENNESSEE
NORTH CAROLINA

129
1
LAKEVIEW DRIVE
3
Deep Creek
19

•Twentymile
2
Fontana Lake

28
•Fontana Village
Bryson City•

74

28

143

Take a Hike

1 Park the car and wander down one of the park's many "Quiet Walkways," quarter-mile paths that give you a closer look at the astounding array of flora and fauna—there are 1,600 species of flowering plants like the fire pink flower (right) in the Smokies. Or you can hit a few of the 800 miles of the park's hiking trails, ranging from a half mile to 70 miles long.

Take a Drive

5 Most visitors to the Great Smoky Mountains area see it by car, taking advantage of the 384 miles of mountain roads lacing the park. Follow the Newfound Gap Road to Clingmans Dome for a vertical journey that takes you to the highest point in the park at 6,643 feet.

Pedal On

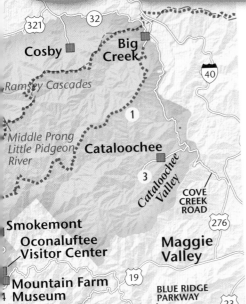

3 Although many park roads are too dangerous—or too steep—for bikes, some, like the 11-mile Cades Cove Loop, are very popular with cyclists. Other areas, such as Greenbrier, Lakeview Drive, Tremont Road, and Cataloochee Valley, are also great places to ride.

Map Labels

321
32
Cosby
Big Creek
Ramsey Cascades
40
Middle Prong Little Pidgeon River
Cataloochee
1
3
Cataloochee Valley
COVE CREEK ROAD
Smokemont
Oconaluftee Visitor Center
276
Maggie Valley
Mountain Farm Museum
19
BLUE RIDGE PARKWAY
23
74

Go Back In Time

4 Stop by the Mountain Farm Museum, adjacent to the Oconaluftee Visitor Center. Learn what life was like there hundreds of years ago by exploring century-old farm buildings (right) and watching demonstrations by park employees, like how the pioneers produced their own cornmeal and flour.

[DARE TO EXPLORE]

PARK IT
About 100 miles northwest of the Great Smoky Mountains in Oneida, Tennessee, is the Big South Fork National River and Recreation Area. Hike, horseback ride, fish, swim, camp, and gawk at waterfalls sure to wow you. **www.nps.gov/biso**

FOREST FUN
Want more wilderness? Chattahoochee National Forest in Gainesville, Georgia (about 95 miles from Great Smoky Mountains), is home to a mix of lakes, streams, valleys, and Brasstown Bald, Georgia's highest mountain at 4,784 feet. Enter the forest's name in the search bar at **www.fs.fed.us.**

WET AND WILD
There are no actual wild bears here—but plenty of wild rides! At the Wild Bear Falls Water Park in Gatlinburg, Tennessee (about 3 miles from Great Smoky Mountains), you can float in an innertube down a lazy river, zoom down slippery slides, and be doused by a huge bucket spilling 300 gallons of water from above! **www.wgwildbearfalls.com**

ALL ABOARD
Climb on the Great Smoky Mountains Railroad in Bryson City, North Carolina. Watch with awe as Western North—and its lush green valleys and river gorges—pass by as you chug along. **www.gsmr.com**

MY CHECKLIST

✓ Hit the hiking trails and check out a waterfall or beautiful trees, plants, and flowers.

✓ Visit the Mountain Farm Museum to learn about life in the Smokies 100 years ago.

✓ Climb to the top of the observation tower on Clingmans Dome.

✓ Go on a bike ride around Cades Cove Loop.

✓ See the Smokies by car on hundreds of miles of mountain roads.

✓ Look for mammals and birds within the Smokies' deciduous forests.

✓ Seek out salamanders in a stream.

FAST FACT: There are more than 2,000 miles of streams in the Smokies.

KE BEAUTIES.

HOT SPRINGS NATIONAL PARK, ARK.

Welcome to Hot Springs National Park!

Not only is Hot Springs one of the country's oldest national parks— it's also the smallest. But what Hot Springs lacks in size it makes up for in character: Set against the backdrop of a mostly urban area, the park is distinguished by its 47 mineral springs, from which a million gallons of thermal (143°F) water spout each day. Whether visitors sip the water or bathe in it, the park's famous hot springs fascinate people from around the world as much today as they did decades ago.

State: Arkansas
Established: March 4, 1921
Size: 5,500 acres
Website: www.nps.gov/hosp

DISCOVER HOT SPRINGS

RANGER TIPS

Drink the water. Tested regularly, the spring water spouting from designated drinking fountains is odorless, fresh tasting, and safe to sip. ⟫

TAKE IT EASY

Dip your toes in the thermal waters as you relax and enjoy the lushness of Arlington Lawn Park in downtown Hot Springs. For a relaxing walk, stroll along the Grand Promenade, a half-mile, landscaped brick walkway that begins behind the Fordyce Bathhouse Visitor Center (below).

BE EXTREME

Visit the Hot Springs pool in Arlington Rock, where you can see and touch the water. Be careful, it's hot! Every year about 700,000 gallons of 143-degree water flow from the springs.

BEST VIEWS

The Hot Springs Mountain observation tower (below) elevates you 1,256 feet above sea level. On a clear day, you can see views extending up to 40 miles on all sides.

ALL ABOUT ANIMALS

Hot Springs National Park is all about amphibians, including toads, salamanders, and frogs. Reptiles, like the ayole lizard (below), live here too. A bevy of birds also call Hot Springs home; keep your eyes peeled for swans, owls, roadrunners, and woodpeckers.

HOT SPRINGS NATIONAL PARK

ARKANSAS

- Ouachita National Forest
- HOT SPRINGS NATIONAL PARK
- Little Rock
- Magic Springs & Crystal Falls
- Crater of Diamonds State Park

Fill Up

2 Take an empty jug to the Thermal Water Jug Fountain on Bathhouse Row and fill it up with fresh-tasting mineral water from the hot springs. Want a cool drink? Take your jug to the Happy Hollow or Whittington cold water springs.

HOT SPRINGS NATIONAL PARK

SUGARLOAF MOUNTAIN

CITY OF HOT SPRINGS

Hot Springs Creek

HOT SPRINGS NATIONAL PARK

Tour the Baths

1 Find out why Hot Springs was once known as the "American Spa" by touring Bathhouse Row, the site of eight bathhouses built in the early 20th century. Start at the Fordyce Bathhouse (left), which serves as the park's visitor center.

3 HOT SPRINGS MOUNTAIN DRIVE

PARK AVENUE

Happy Hollow Spring

AVENUE

WHITTINGTON

DRIVE

7

Arlington Lawn

GRAND PROMENADE

FOUNTAIN ST.

Hot Springs Mt. Tower 1,040 ft

4 PEAK TRAIL

HOT SPRINGS MOUNTAIN

Bathhouse Row

Whittington Spring

2

WEST MOUNTAIN

WEST MOUNTAIN SUMMIT DRIVE

HOT SPRINGS NATIONAL PARK

1,100 ft

1 Fordyce Bathhouse (Visitor Center)

Thermal Water Jug Fountain

City Visitor Center

CITY OF HOT SPRINGS

PROSPECT AVENUE

CENTRAL AVENUE

MALVERN AVENUE

Hot Springs Creek

70

Take a Drive

3 Drive up the winding and scenic Hot Springs and North Mountain Roads to the top of Hot Springs Mountain, where you can catch stunning views from an observation tower.

70 **270**

270

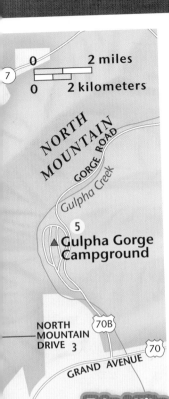

0 ——— 2 miles
0 ——— 2 kilometers

NORTH MOUNTAIN

GORGE ROAD

Gulpha Creek

5
▲ Gulpha Gorge
Campground

NORTH
MOUNTAIN
DRIVE 3

70B

70

GRAND AVENUE

Take a Hike

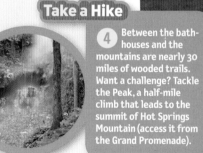

4 Between the bath-houses and the mountains are nearly 30 miles of wooded trails. Want a challenge? Tackle the Peak, a half-mile climb that leads to the summit of Hot Springs Mountain (access it from the Grand Promenade).

Camp Out

5 Pitch a tent and sleep under the stars at Gulpha Gorge Campground (right) next to rushing rapids or a babbling brook.

[DARE TO EXPLORE]

FOLLOW THE FOREST
Explore the nearby Ouachita National Forest, the oldest national forest in the South. About 10 miles west of Hot Springs, you can connect with a mountain road that will lead you to hidden nooks and spectacular views.
fs.usda.gov/ouachita

MAGIC RIDE
Take a dip—and do a flip!—at Magic Springs & Crystal Falls, the only theme park within a national park. Zoom down a waterslide, spin around on a carousel, or zip around on lightning-quick roller coasters and rides. **www.magicsprings.com**

DIAMOND HUNT
Look for a diamond in the rough at Crater of Diamonds State Park in Murfreesboro (about 60 miles from Hot Springs). Scour a plowed field and try to spy diamonds in every color of the rainbow, plus plenty of other precious stones, rocks, and minerals. **www.craterofdiamondsstatepark.com**

SECRET GARDEN
Take a relaxed nature walk through Garvan Woodland botanical gardens, a 210-acre park nestled alongside picturesque Lake Hamilton in Hot Springs. In the spring, follow trails that burst with blooms and trees in every type and color.
www.garvangardens.com

MY CHECKLIST

✓ Take a tour of the historic bath houses on Bathhouse Row.

✓ Stroll down the Grand Promenade.

✓ Camp out or play at Gulpha Gorge Campground.

✓ Get whisked to the top of the Hot Springs Mountain observation tower.

✓ Fill up a jug of hot or cold water straight from the springs.

✓ Look for frogs and other critters in Gulpha Gorge Creek.

✓ Relax in the shade in Arlington Lawn Park.

FAST FACT: Water from the hot springs fell as rain when the pyramids of Egypt were built—4,400 years ago!

◆ Other Must-see Park Properties in the East

ASSATEAGUE ISLAND NATIONAL SEASHORE (MD, VA)

www.nps.gov/asis

WHY IT'S COOL: Wild ponies roam this park's sandy beaches.

WHAT TO DO: Watch for wildlife as you cruise the coastline; swimming, camping, boating, and fishing.

TRY THIS: Climb to the top of the Assateague Lighthouse for sweeping views of the ocean and islands below.

BOSTON NATIONAL HISTORICAL PARK (MA)

www.nps.gov/bost

WHY IT'S COOL: It tells the story of American independence and the Revolutionary War.

WHAT TO DO: Check out Bunker Hill Monument, Faneuil Hall, the Old North Church, the U.S.S. *Constitution*, and the Paul Revere House.

TRY THIS: Take a self-guided adventure along the 2.5-mile Boston Freedom Trail.

CAPE COD NATIONAL SEASHORE (MA)

www.nps.gov/caco

WHY IT'S COOL: It's an "arm" of sandy beaches, wetlands, salt marshes, and woodlands.

WHAT TO DO: Explore historic lighthouses; hiking, biking, swimming, and surfing.

TRY THIS: Watch films about Cape Cod at the Salt Pond Visitor Center.

COLONIAL NATIONAL HISTORICAL PARK (VA)

www.nps.gov/colo

WHY IT'S COOL: It protects the sites of Historic Jamestowne and Yorktown Battlefield.

WHAT TO DO: Tour the park's historic areas and walk or bike the Battlefield Tour roads.

TRY THIS: Join the Pinch Pot Program to learn how Native Americans and English settlers made and used pottery.

DELAWARE WATER GAP NATIONAL RECREATION AREA (NJ, PA)

www.nps.gov/dewa

WHY IT'S COOL: It is home to the Middle Delaware River, one of the cleanest rivers in the U.S., plus plenty of wildlife, waterfalls, and trails.

WHAT TO DO: Swimming, fishing, boating, canoeing, kayaking, rafting, and tubing.

TRY THIS: Check out the world-famous "Water Gap," where the Delaware River cuts through the Appalachian Mountains.

FORT SUMTER NATIONAL MONUMENT (SC)

www.nps.gov/fosu

WHY IT'S COOL: It's the spot where the American Civil War began.

WHAT TO DO: Tour historic forts; boating, fishing, kayaking, and bird-watching.

TRY THIS: Check out the Fort Sumter museum to learn how the fort was built.

GULF ISLANDS NATIONAL SEASHORE (FL, MS)

www.nps.gov/guis

WHY IT'S COOL: This scenic spot offers white sandy beaches, blue water, and glimpses of forts that date back almost 150 years.

WHAT TO DO: Check out historic forts; swimming, snorkeling, fishing, hiking, boating, biking, and strolling along the beach.

TRY THIS: Camp out at Fort Pickens and set out on some of the surrounding scenic hiking trails.

KENNESAW MOUNTAIN NATIONAL BATTLEFIELD PARK (GA)

www.nps.gov/kemo

WHY IT'S COOL: This is where some of the heaviest fighting of the Civil War's Atlanta campaign took place.

WHAT TO DO: Visit battlefields and see monuments to the soldiers who fought here.

TRY THIS: Hike 1.2 miles to the top of Kennesaw Mountain, 1,808 feet above sea level.

NATIONAL MALL AND MEMORIAL PARKS (DC)

www.nps.gov/nacc

WHY IT'S COOL: It is home to famous monuments and museums of our nation's capital.

WHAT TO DO: Check out the Washington Monument, Lincoln Memorial, Vietnam Veterans Memorial, National Air and Space Museum, and Museum of Natural History, among others.

TRY THIS: Paddleboat around the Tidal Basin, then have a picnic on the grassy open space of the National Mall.

SALEM MARITIME NATIONAL HISTORIC SITE (MA)

www.nps.gov/sama

WHY IT'S COOL: It's one of the most important ports in the United States.

WHAT TO DO: Tour Salem Maritime's historic buildings and walk around the city of Salem.

TRY THIS: Visit the *Friendship*, a reconstruction of a 171-foot, three-masted tall ship built in 1797.

STATUE OF LIBERTY NATIONAL MONUMENT (NJ, NY)

www.nps.gov/stli

WHY IT'S COOL: It's the symbol of America to the world.

WHAT TO DO: Visit the Statue of Liberty and explore Ellis Island's museum of immigration.

TRY THIS: Join the park rangers for a free 30-minute outdoor tour.

WRIGHT BROTHERS NATIONAL MEMORIAL (NC)

www.nps.gov/wrbr

WHY IT'S COOL: It's the site of the first powered flight.

WHAT TO DO: Visit the spot where the Wright brothers first took off and landed; tour the park's museums and exhibits.

TRY THIS: Participate in programs like "Fun in Flight," in which you create your own paper airplane.

the Midwest

Theodore Roosevelt National Park

A herd of beautiful wild horses runs across the wide open spaces of Theodore Roosevelt National Park in North Dakota.

the Midwest

NESTLED IN BETWEEN the Appalachians and the Rocky Mountains, the Midwest parks offer a variety pack of landscapes, from the grand Great Lakes to the sweeping sandstone cliffs of the badlands. Mile upon mile of prairies and cornfields make up most of the Midwest, and the area's national parks let you roam free among these seemingly endless grasslands. The spirit of America's frontier is preserved in the rugged scenery and untouched acres that are show-cased in the Midwest national parks.

That's not to say the Midwest is all fields and flow-ers—it is also home to urban national parks, including Jefferson National Expansion Memorial in St. Louis (where you'll find the Gateway Arch) and Cuyahoga Valley near Cleveland, Ohio (visit waterfalls galore!). These areas are incredibly rich in history—one park, for example, traces the route taken by the Lewis and Clark expedi-tion to the Pacific Ocean in the early 1800s, and another is named in honor of President Theodore Roosevelt, who became enchanted with this unique area back in 1883.

And if that's not enough, there are ancient rock formations to gawk at and a massive network of under-ground passages to explore. Not to mention there's plenty of wildlife, too: Deer, pronghorn, bison, reptiles, and of course the prairie dog can all be spotted during your visit to the Midwest.

MAP KEY

BADLANDS NATIONAL PARK Bold, uppercase type indicates featured park in the Midwest section.

CANADA
U.S.

Voyageurs N.P.

Isle Royale N.P.

Lake Superior

MINNESOTA

WISCONSIN

MICHIGAN

Lake Michigan

Lake Huron

Minneapolis
St. Paul

Mississippi

Detroit

Lake Erie

PA.

IOWA

Chicago

Cleveland

CUYAHOGA NATIONAL PARK

OHIO

ILLINOIS

INDIANA

Ohio

WEST VIRGINIA

Missouri

St. Louis

Lexington

MISSOURI

KENTUCKY

Mammoth Cave N.P.

VIRGINIA

Ohio

Arkansas

TENNESSEE

NORTH CAROLINA

Nashville

Great Smoky Mountains National Park

OKLAHOMA

ARKANSAS

SOUTH CAROLINA

Hot Springs National Park

Little Rock

Atlanta

Mississippi

ALABAMA

GEORGIA

MISSISSIPPI

0   300 miles

0   300 kilometers

LOUISIANA

FLORIDA

37

Welcome to Badlands National Park!

Early French-Canadian trappers named it *les mauvaises terres à traverser.* Translation? "Bad lands to cross." But there's nothing bad to say about this extremely unique region. Famous for its towering, jagged cliffs, steep-walled canyons, and bumpy gray terrain, the rocky landscape of Badlands National Park is

State: South Dakota
Established: November 10, 1978
Size: 244,300 acres
Website: www.nps.gov/badl

often compared to the moon's surface. But the park is also home to Buffalo Gap National Grassland, the largest mixed-grass prairie in the National Park System. The combination of distinct rock formations and lush grasslands makes Badlands one of the most beautiful and bizarre places in the world.

DISCOVER BADLANDS

RANGER TIPS

Don't get too close to the edge of any overlooks or trails; the loose ground may erode beneath your feet. Find a fossil? Don't touch it, and report it to the visitor center.

TAKE IT EASY

Go for a walk on the park's many trails (center) or in the mixed-grass prairie, where you'll wander through both ankle-high and waist-high grasses (top).

BE EXTREME

Up for a climb? Parts of the 1.5-mile Notch Trail are so steep, you have to scale a log ladder to reach higher ground. Reach the top and be rewarded with sweeping views of the White River Valley basin.

BEST VIEWS

Head to Big Badlands Overlook for an outstanding aerial view of The Wall and glimpses of the cliffs and grassy prairie (below). The Cliff Shelf Nature Trail also offers a spectacular view of the plains.

ALL ABOUT ANIMALS

Park residents include pronghorn, mule and whitetail deer, prairie dogs (below), coyotes, butterflies, turtles, snakes, bluebirds, vultures, eagles, and hawks. Bonus points if you spot the once endangered bison, bighorn sheep, swift fox, and black-footed ferret, all species recently reintroduced to Badlands.

Take a Tour

1 Visit the Ben Reifel Visitor Center (left) for an overview on everything the area has to offer, from its geological past to its current wildlife. Don't miss the film "Land of Stone and Light."

Take a Hike

2 From the Ben Reifel Visitor Center, start down one of the eight nearby trails, which range from easy jaunts to longer treks. You'll walk by Badlands' most amazing formations, like The Wall, a long, narrow spine of buttes (right) stretching for 60 miles.

44

Roberts Prairie Dog Town

240

SAGE CREEK RIM ROAD

4

590

BADLANDS NATIONAL PARK

NORTH UNIT

B A D L A N D S

Scenic

BUFFALO GAP NATIONAL GRASSLAND

44

BUFFALO GAP NATIONAL GRASSLAND

589

40

Cheyenne River

Red Shirt

41

27

BADLANDS NATIONAL PARK STRONGHOLD UNIT (SOUTH UNIT)

0   4 miles

0   4 kilometers

SOUTH DAKOTA

Keystone   ●Pierre

BADLANDS NATIONAL PARK

●Hot Springs

White River

PALMER CREEK UNIT

 White River Visitor Center

2

2

41

23

27

Take a Drive

3 Situated just ten minutes off the interstate, Badlands is superaccessible by car. Follow the 25-mile Badlands Loop (left) and watch eroded buttes, pinnacles, spires, and grasslands pass by your window.

5 Follow the quarter-mile Fossil Exhibit Trail and find out about the extinct animals that once roamed the badlands, from three-toed horses to saber-toothed cats (left). If you're lucky, you may be able to watch paleontologists prospecting for prehistoric bones.

[DARE TO EXPLORE]

HEADS UP
Two hours from Badlands, near Keystone, South Dakota, looms Mount Rushmore National Memorial, the iconic landmark featuring the heads of four former U.S. Presidents carved in the side of a mountain. Take the half-mile-long Presidential Trail to look up the noses of the Presidents and stay until sunset for the lighting ceremony. **www.nps.gov/mor**

GO CRAZY
Travel two hours from Badlands to Crazy Horse, South Dakota, home to the Crazy Horse Memorial. This mountain-size statue of a Lakota Indian riding a horse has been under construction for more than 60 years and is as long as a cruise ship and taller than a 60-story skyscraper! Visit the Indian Museum of North America and learn to grind corn and make crafts just like the Lakota Indians did. **www.crazyhorsememorial.org**

FOSSIL FUN
Twenty-six thousand years ago, Columbian and woolly mammoths became trapped in a sinkhole and died. Today, you can visit that spot in Hot Springs, South Dakota, known as Mammoth Site (about 2.5 hours from Badlands). Watch fossils being uncovered, explore a hut made out of mammoth bones, and learn more about prehistoric creatures. **www.mammothsite.com**

TAKE THE PLUNGE
After you leave Mammoth Site, put on your bathing suit and make a stop at Evans Plunge, a waterpark filled with water from a natural hot spring. Soak or splash in the warm water or shoot down your choice of three slides. **www.evansplunge.com**

Map

UFFALO GAP
NATIONAL
GRASSLAND
Cactus Flat
90
BADLANDS **3**
LOOP ROAD
240 Big Badlands Overlook
Fossil Exhibit Trail **5** NORTH UNIT
V A L L
NotchTrail
Cliff Shelf Trail
2
Interior **377** **1** Ben Reifel Visitor Center

Watch Wildlife

4 Grab your binoculars and head down Sage Creek Rim Road into the park's wilderness area. You may spot buffalo (left), pronghorn, and bighorn sheep roaming the grasslands.

MY CHECKLIST

✓ DRIVE THE BADLANDS LOOP ROAD.

✓ SIGN UP FOR A RANGER-LED PROGRAM LIKE THE GEOLOGY WALK OR FOSSIL TALK.

✓ HIKE ONE OF BADLAND'S BEST TRAILS, SUCH AS THE DOOR TRAIL OR THE MORE STRENUOUS CLIFF SHELF TRAIL.

✓ CHECK OUT THE EXHIBITS AT THE VISITOR CENTER.

✓ FOLLOW THE FOSSIL EXHIBIT TRAIL TO LEARN ABOUT THE PREHISTORIC CREATURES THAT LIVED IN THE AREA.

✓ ATTEND A NIGHT SKY PROGRAM AND VIEW THE SPARKLING NIGHT SKY THROUGH A TELESCOPE.

✓ LOOK FOR WILDLIFE ROAMING IN THE PRAIRIES.

FAST FACT: Badlands National Park is considered to be one of the world's richest deposits of mammal fossil beds.

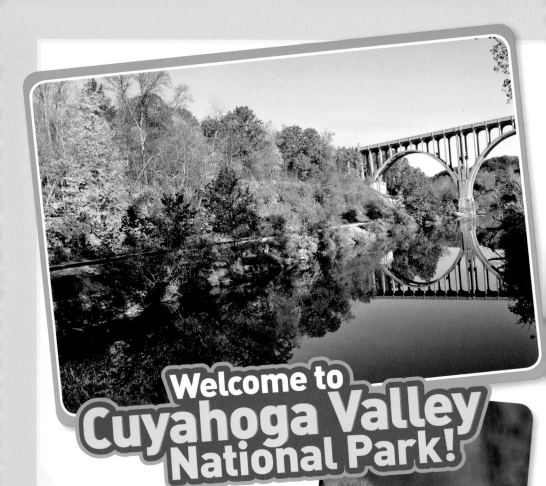

Welcome to Cuyahoga Valley National Park!

SQUIRREL

Between the bustling cities of Cleveland and Akron, Ohio, lies Cuyahoga Valley, a haven of quiet trails, tree-covered hills, and pockets of wild greenery. Visitors can follow the park's 20-mile towpath along the banks of the Ohio & Erie Canal, spy beavers on the river, gather at a music center for outdoor concerts in the summer, or ride sleds down its hills in the winter. Plus, the park's many waterfalls, abundance of plants, and variety of trees make it one of the region's most beautiful areas—and a true treasure in the state of Ohio.

State: Ohio
Established: October 11, 2000
Size: 33,000 acres
Website: www.nps.gov/cuva

DISCOVER CUYAHOGA VALLEY

BEST VIEWS

Check out Tinkers Creek Gorge, a national natural landmark that offers an overlook with an amazing view of the wooded valley and creek, 200 feet below. At dusk, scale Ledges Overlook for stunning and colorful sunset views over wooded ridges as far as the eye can see. For a view of one of the prettiest waterfalls in the park, head down the trail leading to Blue Hen Falls (left).

RANGER TIPS

Ask about ranger-led tours and special events at the Canal Visitor Center. The best times to tour Cuyahoga? Spring (for the wildflowers, right) and fall (for the foliage).

TAKE IT EASY

Hit the trails (below) for a fun and easy adventure or visit the Happy Days Lodge, a center hosting concerts, dances, and kids' activities. Check with the visitor center for a schedule of events. For a step back in time, visit the Hale Farm & Village, where you can see what life was like in the Cuyahoga Valley in the 1800s.

BE EXTREME

Visiting in the winter? Cross-country ski past ponds, down steep hills, and along the Ohio & Erie Canal. You can also opt to sled, snow tube, snowshoe, or downhill ski at nearby resorts. When you're done with your extreme adventure check out the swirling wintertime icicles formed by frozen waterfalls.

ALL ABOUT ANIMALS

The unique urban location of Cuyahoga Valley makes the park a refuge for a variety of animals. Explore the park's trails and wetland habitats to see deer, squirrels, beavers, and birds like the belted kingfisher (below), great blue heron, red-winged blackbird, and bald eagle.

Ride the Rails

1 The Cuyahoga Valley Scenic Railroad (below) parallels the river and makes seven stops within the park. Get off at the Canal Visitor Center or the Village of Peninsula and then hop back on the train to return to your original station.

Follow the Falls

2 Take in the amazing sight that is Brandywine Falls (right), a 65-foot cascade that turns into a thundering spectacle when water levels are high. Check it out at three different vantage points, each accessible by a walkway.

Explore the Past

3 Stop by the Boston Store, a historic building where settlers in the 1800s bought and sold goods with merchants traveling the Ohio & Erie Canal (left). Exhibits tell the story of canalboat-building in the valley.

ROCKSIDE RD.
77
21
TINKERS CREEK ROAD
Bedford
TOWPATH TRAIL
CANAL ROAD
TINKERS CREEK GORGE
Rang
GORGE PARKWAY
Independence
Canal Visitor Center
1
Tinkers Creek
ALEXANDER ROAD
PLEASANT VALLEY ROAD
Cuyahoga River
CANALWAY OHIO NATIONAL SCENIC BYWAY
8
77
1
Northfield
CUYAHOGA VALLEY SCENIC RAILROAD
CUYAHOGA
Brecksville
82
Sagamore Hills
82
Ranger Station
RIVERVIEW RD.
BRANDYWINE ROAD
77
VALLEY
OHIO & ERIE CANAL TOWPATH TRAIL
80
Ranger Station
2
Bran Falls
FURNACE RUN
21
80
3
Boston Store
Blue Hen Falls
NATIONAL
Peninsula Depot Visitor Center
1
Richfield
Peninsula
303
5
CANALWAY OHIO NATIONAL SCENIC BYWAY
Ritchi Ledges & Ice Box Cav
271
77
PARK
Everett Road Covered Bridge
4
Ranger Station
Hunt Farm Visitor Center
OHIO & ERIE CAN TOWPATH TRAIL
4
AKRON PENINSUL ROAD
0   1 miles
0   1 kilometers
Cuyahoga River

[DARE TO EXPLORE]

GET WILD

Transport yourself from the forest to the rain forest—and beyond—with a stop at Cleveland Metroparks Zoo & Forest, a 30-minute drive from the park. Be wowed by more than 600 animals and insects from seven continents and a newly opened 5-acre elephant exhibit. **www.clemetzoo.com**

HISTORIC HOUSE

Plan a stop at the James A. Garfield National Historic Site in Mentor, Ohio (about 30 miles from Cuyahoga). Tour the home of Garfield, the 20th President of the United States, and learn about his life and work. For some quiet time, stroll the home's tranquil grounds and peaceful paths. **www.nps.gov/jaga**

MUSIC MUSEUM

Spend an afternoon in Cleveland's Rock and Roll Hall of Fame. Dedicated to all things rock and roll, you can listen to music, check out crazy costumes, and see what being a rock star is really like. About 30 minutes from the park. **www.rockhall.com**

THRILL TIME

Up your thrill factor at Cedar Point and Soak City, home to oodles of crazy-fun rides, like the Dragster, a 120-mph roller coaster that zooms 420 feet up in the air. In Sandusky, Ohio (about 65 miles from Cuyahoga). **www.cedarpoint.com**

Bike It

4 Pedal along the Ohio & Erie Canal Towpath Trail (below). Shady and flat, the trail rolls for about 20 miles in the park beside the Cuyahoga River, past marshes, and through the Everett Road Covered Bridge.

Rock Stars

5 Rock 320 million years old forms the 105-foot-high Ritchie Ledges (right). Stand in the shadows of these blocks of orange and yellow rock, then explore nearby Ice Box Cave, a 50-foot-deep, narrow slit in the rock where the temperature stays cool year round.

MY CHECKLIST

✓ Stop by the visitor center for fun exhibits and info on the park.

✓ Walk or bike the Towpath Trail.

✓ Take a ride on the Cuyahoga Valley Scenic Railroad.

✓ Visit Lock 38, the last working canal lock within the park.

✓ Explore Ritchie Ledges and Ice Box Cave.

✓ Climb to the top of Brandywine Falls.

✓ In the winter, tour the park by sled, snow tube, skis, or snowshoes.

FAST FACT: This national park is home to more than 60 waterfalls.

Lake Erie

Sandusky • • Cleveland
CUYAHOGA NATIONAL PARK • Akron

O H I O

◉ Columbus

cedonia

ndywine Creek

80
8

appy Days isitor enter

edges Overlook

ENDALL ARK OAD

Welcome to Theodore Roosevelt National Park!

Theodore Roosevelt National Park is named for the President

who became enchanted with this unique area back in 1883—then went on to establish five national parks and help found the U.S. Forest Service. Known for its rugged terrain, the park began forming its unique landscape 65 million years ago. Today the park is home to a rich variety of wildlife and includes both the Little Missouri River and the Little Missouri badlands; it is divided into two parts (the South and North Units). Its unrivaled array of jagged cliffs, steep slopes, rounded hills, and springtime wildflowers spreading vivid colors throughout the prairies make Theodore Roosevelt a one-of-a-kind destination.

State: North Dakota
Established: November 10, 1978
Size: 70,447 acres
Website: www.nps.gov/thro

🚙 DISCOVER THEODORE ROOSEVELT 🚙

RANGER TIPS

Keep your distance from bison; they are quick and may attack if approached. Make sure to also keep an eye out for rattlesnakes and black widow spiders, which often live in prairie dog burrows. And don't feed the prairie dogs—they bite!

TAKE IT EASY

On clear nights, you can *almost* see forever (above). So head to the park after dark, lie back, and look for planets, stars, constellations, and maybe even a meteor shower! ☁

BE EXTREME

Hop on a horse and gallop down some of the Maah Daah Hey Trail (above), which at one point crosses over the Little Missouri River. ☁

BEST VIEWS

In the South Unit, pull off at the North Dakota Badlands Overlook for an amazing look at the area around you. In the North Unit, the River Bend Overlook offers a stunning vista of the Little Missouri River (below) and badlands on either side. ☁

ALL ABOUT ANIMALS

Look for prairie dogs (below) along the Scenic Loop Drive (and listen for their telltale chirp as they warn each other of your arrival). You may also see beavers in the river and white-tailed deer, bison, elk, antelope, and wild horses grazing on the grassy plateaus. And watch for birds, too. There are more than 186 types of birds that either live in or pass through the park! ☁

2 At the visitor center in Medora, don't miss the Maltese Cross Cabin (below), which once served as the headquarters of Roosevelt's first cattle ranch. The cabin is complete with the original furniture and some of Roosevelt's personal belongings, such as his traveling trunk, inscribed with his initials.

Take a Hike

3 Follow the Ridgeline Nature Trail and the Coal Vein Trail, both self-guided nature trails that offer lessons on the environment around you.

Take a Drive

1 The 36-mile Scenic Loop Drive in the South Unit and the 14-mile drive in the North Unit (below) provide easy access to vistas and wildlife spotting. Look out your window and see bison and prairie dog towns; park the car at a turnout and gawk at the amazingly unique landscape.

SCENIC DRIVE

0 — 1 mile
0 — 1 kilometer

River Bend Overlook

THEODORE ROOSEVELT

Little Missouri River

Oxbow Overlook

NATIONAL PARK

NORTH UNIT

B A D L A N D S

LITTLE MISSOURI NATIONAL GRASSLAND

MAAH DAAH HEY TRAIL

THEODORE ROOSEVELT NATIONAL PARK

Knife River Indian Villages N.H.S

NORTH DAKOTA
Bismarck

Lake Ilo N.W.R.

Little Missouri River

WIND CANYON TRAIL

B A

SCENIC LOOP DRIVE

MAAH DAAH HEY TRAIL

Wind Canyon Overlook

Prairie Dog Town

THEODORE ROOSEVEL

LITTLE MISSOURI NATIONAL GRASSLAND

Cottonwood Campground **4**

1

NATIONAL PAR

Prairie Dog Town

North Dakota Badlan Overlo

94

Skyline Vista

SCENIC LOOP DRIVE

RIDGELINE TRAIL

Medora Visitor Center (Maltese Cross Cabin)

2 **5**

3

Medora

Medora Children's Park

94

MAAH DAAH HEY TRAIL

0 — 2 mile
0 — 2 kilometer

Sully Creek State Primitive Park

North Unit Visitor Center

SCENIC DRIVE

Longhorn Pullout

△ CCC Campground

Camp Out

4 Pitch a tent in Cottonwood Campground, near the banks of the Little Missouri River, which winds through Wind Canyon (right). Plopped in the middle of the wilderness, you're bound to have a close encounter with wildlife ... and just may wake up in the morning to find bison tracks outside your site.

...TLE MISSOURI NATIONAL GRASSLAND

Family Fun

5 Head to the Medora Visitor Center or the North Unit Visitor Center to borrow a Family Fun Pack. For 24 hours, you'll be loaned field guides, binoculars, hand lenses, and activities to help make your visit even more exciting.

SOUTH UNIT

△ *Buck Hill* 2,855 ft
COAL VEIN TRAIL

Painted Canyon Visitor Center

94

[DARE TO EXPLORE]

GO TO THE GRASSLAND
Spot more wildlife at the Little Missouri National Grassland, where bighorn sheep, elk, pronghorn, hawks, and grouse live. You can also camp, hike, and horseback ride in this protected prairie surrounding Theodore Roosevelt National Park.
www.fs.fed.us/r1/dakotaprairie

SEEK REFUGE
Boat, fish, picnic, and take in stunning sights at Lake Ilo National Wildlife Refuge, about 50 miles east of Theodore Roosevelt National Park.
www.fws.gov/lakeilo

PLAY TIME
Make believe you're back in the Wild West at Medora Children's Park. Play in an Old West fort, a stagecoach, and an old-fashioned train engine. Located near the national park's headquarters in Medora. **www.medora.com**

GO TRIBAL
Make a stop at the Knife River Indian Villages National Historic Site, about 130 miles east of Theodore Roosevelt. You'll see the remains of Native American villages, once home to thriving civilizations. An on-site museum highlights the colorful culture of the local tribes that have lived on the land for more than 11,000 years.
www.nps.gov/knri

MY CHECKLIST

✔ Check out Roosevelt's belongings at the Maltese Cross Cabin.

✔ Go on a bike ride on one of the park's paved or dirt roads.

✔ Hike some of the many self-guided trails in the park.

✔ Take in a view of the Little Missouri River.

✔ Soak in the sights from the car on the drive along Scenic Loop.

✔ Sleep under the stars at Cottonwood Campground.

✔ Pick up a Family Fun Pack at the visitor center.

FAST FACT: Fifty-five million years ago, the Dakota plains were a swamp similar to southern Louisiana.

Welcome to Wind Cave National Park!

Tucked in between the Black Hills National Forest and the windswept North Dakota prairie, Wind Cave is a blend of both dense woods and wide-open grasslands. But the true gem of this park is actually something you can't see—unless you travel underground. Discovered by two brothers in 1881, Wind Cave features 130 miles of underground passages, making it one of the world's longest caves. In the caves, you will see many bizarre mineral formations, including honeycomb-like structures called boxwork. Listen closely and you just may hear a whistling noise—that's the sound of the strong winds that rush in and out of the cave's mouth, giving the park its name.

State: South Dakota
Established: January 9, 1903
Size: 28,295 acres
Website: www.nps.gov/wica

DISCOVER WIND CAVE

RANGER TIPS

Don't rely on cell phones to stay in touch; coverage is spotty within Wind Cave. You should also be prepared for severe thunderstorms and occasional hail, most common in the summer. And bring a light sweater or jacket: The caves are only 53°F year-round.

TAKE IT EASY

Need a break? Grab some snacks, spread out a blanket, and relax at the designated picnic areas near the visitor center and Elk Mountain Campground. If you're in the mood for a walk, enjoy the beautiful rolling prairies (top) or take the Garden of Eden tour, an easy one-hour loop.

BE EXTREME

Delve deep into Wind Cave on the four-hour Wild Cave Tour (below). Crawl through narrow openings, squeeze into tight passages, and get dirty as you scramble into the far reaches of this massive cave. (Note: The minimum age for the Wild Cave Tour is 16, and the park requires a signed consent form for those 17 and under.)

BEST VIEW

From the Rankin Ridge Trail, take a 1-mile walk among the Ponderosa pines (above) to a fire tower. You can climb partway up the tower for a great view of the surrounding landscape.

ALL ABOUT ANIMALS

Take a walk around and you're bound to see pronghorn (below), mule deer, and prairie dogs scampering about in the open grasslands. Bison also roam here. And because of the park's small size and relatively large bison population, your chances of seeing them are pretty good! Also look for elk (you might spot some on the outer edges of the forests), red-tailed hawks, golden eagles, bats, insects, and fish.

5 Stop by the Life in the Prairie Dog Town to check out the rodents roaming in their natural habitat. Hear that high-pitched bark? That's how prairie dogs warn each other of your arrival.

Map 1 (Wind Cave National Park overview)

CUSTER STATE PARK

RANKIN RIDGE TRAIL

5

SCENIC DRIVE

3

WIND CAVE

NATIONAL PARK

6

87

4 → HIGHLAND CREEK TRAIL

385

5 ■ Praire Dog Town
▲ Elk Mountain Campground

ELK MOUNTAIN TRAIL

■ Visitor Center

Beaver Creek

5

385

101

0 — 2 mi
0 — 2 km

Tour Legend

- — — Natural Entrance Tour
- ——— Fairgrounds Tour
- ——— Candlelight Tour

Map 2 (Cave interior)

Devil's Tower Nat. Mon. ■
WYOMING
SOUTH DAKOTA
Michelson ● Pierre Trail
WIND CAVE NATIONAL PARK
■ Buffalo Gap National Grassland

2

Bachelo Quarter

Pearly Gates

Fairgrounds 3,967 ft

Standing Rock Chamber

Elks Room 3,911 ft

Elevator Building 4,055 ft

1

Temple Room

Crossroads 3,885 ft

Methodist Church

Assembly Room 3,863 ft

North Room 3,983 ft

Post Office 3,960 ft

Devil's Lookout 3,931 ft

Roe's Misery

Parking Area

Visitor Center 4,095 ft

N

Cave Entrance 4,082 ft

Parking Area

0 — 400 feet
0 — 100 meters

2 Join the Candlelight Tour, a two-hour candlelit exploration of Wind Cave that transports you back to the 1890s, when tours were measured by the number of candles needed to complete them. Make sure you look out for the unique boxwork formations (right)! (Note: You must be eight years old to take the Candlelight Tour.)

4 There are plenty of hikes in the park, from the easy, 1-mile Elk Mountain Nature Trail, where you can learn about the park's plants, like prickly pear cactus (right), to the longer 7.3-mile Highland Creek Trail, which takes you past a huge prairie dog colony.

[DARE TO EXPLORE]

PARK HOP

Take time to visit the adjacent Custer State Park. The 1,500-strong bison herd is one of the largest in the world. Also nearby? Buffalo Gap National Grassland (about 75 miles from Wind Cave), where you can hike, mountain bike, or camp among the mix of grasslands and badlands. **www.gfp.sd.gov/state-parks/directory/custer** (Custer); **(605) 279-2125** (Buffalo Gap)

EXPLORE MORE

Can't get enough of caving? Travel to Custer, South Dakota, about 35 miles northwest of Wind Cave, to see Jewel Cave National Monument. This 142-mile-long cave features calcite crystals that sparkle like jewels. **(605) 673-2288**

TERRIFIC TOWER

Make your way to Devils Tower, which became the country's first national monument in 1906. Rising 1,267 feet above the Belle Fourche River, you can explore the tower—and the surrounding park packed with plenty of plants and wildlife. Located in Devils Tower, Wyoming, about 130 miles from Wind Cave. **www.nps.gov/deto**

TOP TRAIL

Bike or hike down the George S. Mickelson Trail, in the heart of the Black Hills. Pass through national forestland, over railroad bridges and through four rock tunnels. Or opt to take the trolley on the trail, a four-hour ride along the 109-mile path. **www.gfp.sd.gov/state-parks/directory/mickelson-trail**

Take a Tour

1 Stop by the visitor center to watch the film "Wind Cave: One Park, Two Worlds," which narrates details about the park's history and unusual ecosystem. From there, you can take the Natural Entrance Tour or the Fairgrounds Tour—both introduce you to the underground world of caves.

Take a Drive

3 Explore the park's prairies and forests from your car by following the Scenic Drive. See some stunning views, spot bison and pronghorn grazing on grass, and stop at one of the many pullouts to learn more about the park's ecology.

MY CHECKLIST

- ✓ Explore Wind Cave.
- ✓ Stop by the visitor center to learn about cave exploration.
- ✓ Join a ranger-led tour.
- ✓ Take a scenic drive to see all of the sights.
- ✓ Camp out at Elk Mountain Campground.
- ✓ Look for wildlife roaming the park's grassy plains.
- ✓ Stay past sunset to stargaze or join in the nightly campfire talk.

FAST FACT: Wind Cave is the world's fourth largest cave.

⏩ Other Must-see Park Properties in the Midwest

AGATE FOSSIL BEDS NATIONAL MONUMENT (NE)

www.nps.gov/agfo

WHY IT'S COOL: It's an essential site for the study of ancient mammals and Native American artifacts.

WHAT TO DO: View the Cook Collection of American Indian Artifacts and the fossils of ancient mammals, hike the Niobrara River Valley.

TRY THIS: Hike to the top of 40-foot-high Agate Falls on the middle branch of the Ontonagon River.

APOSTLE ISLANDS NATIONAL LAKESHORE (WI)

www.nps.gov/apis

WHY IT'S COOL: You won't believe the beauty of the park's 21 Lake Superior islands and 12 miles of shoreline.

WHAT TO DO: Visit historic lighthouses; hiking, boating, sailing, cruising, camping, fishing, and scuba diving.

TRY THIS: Launch a kayak from Meyers Beach and explore mainland sea caves.

ICE AGE NATIONAL SCENIC TRAIL (WI)

www.nps.gov/iatr

WHY IT'S COOL: The trail traces the edge of an ancient glacier, offering views of cool geological formations.

WHAT TO DO: Hiking, backpacking, camping, bird-watching, stargazing, and snowshoeing.

TRY THIS: Visiting in the winter? Strap on some cross-country skis and hit some of the park's 1,200 miles of trails.

JEFFERSON NATIONAL EXPANSION MEMORIAL (IL, MO)

www.nps.gov/jeff

WHY IT'S COOL: Its centerpiece is the 630-foot-tall Gateway Arch in St. Louis, the tallest man-made monument in the United States.

WHAT TO DO: Visit the arch, explore the riverfront area by bike, and visit the Museum of Westward Expansion.

TRY THIS: Take a tram ride to the top of the arch for sweeping views of the St. Louis area.

LEWIS & CLARK NATIONAL HISTORIC TRAIL (IL, MO, KS, IA, ME, SD, ND, MT, ID, OR, WA)

www.nps.gov/lecl

WHY IT'S COOL: It's the route taken by the Lewis and Clark expedition in its search for a water route to the Pacific Ocean between 1804 and 1806.

WHAT TO DO: Retrace the expedition's path by car, bicycle, or boat; skiing or snowshoeing in the winter; rafting or canoeing the Missouri River.

TRY THIS: Hike Idaho's Bitterroot Mountains in the footsteps of early American explorers.

MISSISSIPPI NATIONAL RIVER AND RECREATION AREA (MN)

www.nps.gov/miss

WHY IT'S COOL: This 72-mile stretch of America's iconic river is home to St. Anthony Falls (the Mississippi's only major waterfall) and Stone Arch Bridge (a national engineering landmark).

WHAT TO DO: Visit museums and historic sites; boating, canoeing, hiking, biking, camping, picnicking, wildlife-watching, cross-country skiing, and snowshoeing.

TRY THIS: Hop on a bike and ride a portion of the 3,000-mile-long Mississippi River Trail.

MOUNT RUSHMORE NATIONAL MEMORIAL (SD)

www.nps.gov/moru/index.htm

WHY IT'S COOL: It features huge sculptures of the heads of former U.S. Presidents.

WHAT TO DO: Go on a ranger-led walk to the base of the carving, then take a Sculptor's Studio Tour to check out the cool tools they use.

TRY THIS: Visit nearby Jewel Cave (the second longest cave in the world) to see cool cave formations.

OZARK NATIONAL SCENIC RIVERWAYS NATIONAL RIVER (MO)

www.nps.gov/ozar

WHY IT'S COOL: Home to two of America's clearest and most beautiful spring-fed rivers, it's also the first national park area to protect a wild river system.

WHAT TO DO: Watch traditional Ozarks craft and skills demonstrations; canoeing, kayaking, inner-tubing, hiking, and horseback riding.

TRY THIS: Explore life beneath the Earth's surface at Ozark Caverns in Lake of the Ozarks State Park.

PICTURED ROCKS NATIONAL LAKESHORE (MI)

www.nps.gov/piro

WHY IT'S COOL: It offers natural beauty along 40 miles of Lake Superior shoreline, including waterfalls, cliffs, beaches, and sand dunes.

WHAT TO DO: Visit the Grand Sable Banks and Dunes; view the Pictured Rocks; hiking, camping, backpacking, bicycling, boating, kayaking, skiing, and snowmobiling.

TRY THIS: On a hot day, take a chilly dip in the clean and clear waters of Lake Superior or just hang out on the lakeshore's white-sand beaches.

SLEEPING BEAR DUNES NATIONAL LAKESHORE (MI)

www.nps.gov/slbe

WHY IT'S COOL: Thirty-five miles of Lake Michigan coastline plus the North and South Manitou Islands make up this site.

WHAT TO DO: Visit the U.S. Coast Guard Museum; check out the South Manitou Island Lighthouse; tour historic sites; swimming, hiking, kayaking, and canoeing.

TRY THIS: Climb the Sleeping Bear Dunes, check out views of Glen Lake, then run down to the picnic area to recharge before you climb again.

TALLGRASS PRAIRIE NATIONAL PRESERVE (KS)

www.nps.gov/tapr

WHY IT'S COOL: It protects a remnant of the threatened tallgrass prairie.

WHAT TO DO: Hiking, wildlife-watching, and fishing.

TRY THIS: Tour the preserve's backcountry while learning about the prairie's plants, animals, and geology on a ranger-led prairie bus tour.

Carlsbad Caverns National Park

Stunning stalactite formations cover the ceiling of an underground chamber in Carlsbad Caverns.

the Southwest

the Southwest

THOUSANDS OF YEARS AGO, an ancient sea sculpted the landscapes of the Southwest. This resulted in a wide range of dazzling scenery seen in the Southwest's national parks, including amazing mountain chains, cool dark caverns, dramatic canyons, a flowing river, and rolling dunes of sand. With such diversity to its landscapes, the Southwest holds the potential for plenty of fun wherever you go, whether hiking a mountain trail, shooting down river rapids, exploring canyons and caves, or taking a spin along one of the area's many scenic drives.

Depending on the yearly precipitation, the Southwest is either awash with brilliant blossoms, like the gorgeous Texas bluebonnets, red and orange cactus flowers, and white yucca blooms, or covered by cacti and other plants that thrive in a parched terrain, like the prickly pear.

This varied climate and topography brings a world of wildlife to the Southwest; it's not unusual to see lizards skittering or snakes slithering along the many trails dissecting the parks. In fact, animals have been roaming this land long before humans, as evident in the many dinosaur fossils found by paleontologists in the Southwest, including the Big Bend pterosaur, the largest animal ever to fly.

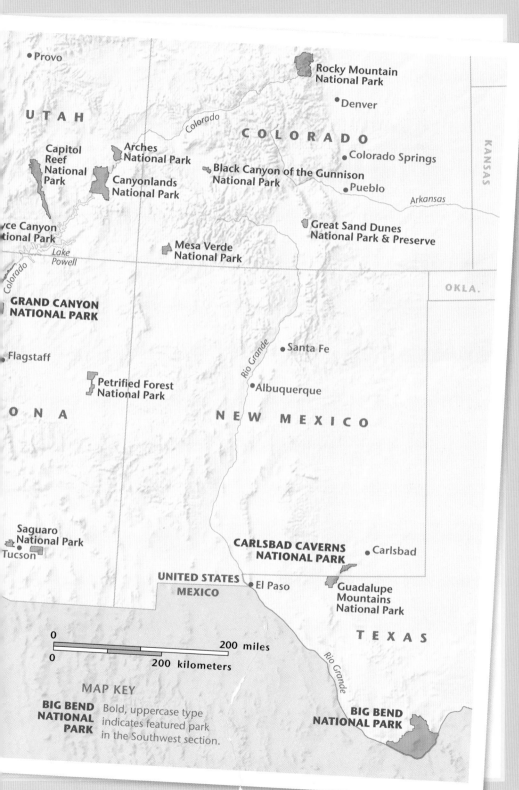

• Provo

Rocky Mountain
National Park

• Denver

U T A H

Colorado

C O L O R A D O

Capitol
Reef
National
Park

Arches
National Park

Canyonlands
National Park

Black Canyon of the Gunnison
National Park

• Colorado Springs

KANSAS

• Pueblo

Arkansas

ce Canyon
ional Park

Lake
Powell

Great Sand Dunes
National Park & Preserve

Colorado

Mesa Verde
National Park

OKLA.

GRAND CANYON
NATIONAL PARK

• Flagstaff

Rio Grande

• Santa Fe

Petrified Forest
National Park

• Albuquerque

O N A

N E W   M E X I C O

Saguaro
National Park

Tucson

CARLSBAD CAVERNS
NATIONAL PARK

• Carlsbad

UNITED STATES
MEXICO

• El Paso

Guadalupe
Mountains
National Park

T E X A S

Rio Grande

| 0 | | 200 miles |
| 0 | | 200 kilometers |

MAP KEY

BIG BEND
NATIONAL
PARK

Bold, uppercase type
indicates featured park
in the Southwest section.

BIG BEND
NATIONAL PARK

Welcome to Big Bend National Park!

Rugged. Remote. Dry. Undisturbed.

These are just some of the words typically used to describe Big Bend National Park, located on the international boundary between the United States and Mexico. Offering stretches of sandy deserts, sun-splashed canyons, towering mountains, and the flowing waters of the Rio Grande, Big Bend is often referred to as "three parks in one." The wide range of landscape offers many trails, a variety of wildlife, and photo ops everywhere you roam. So regardless of how remote Big Bend may be, you'll always have plenty to keep you occupied—and amazed.

State: Texas
Established: June 12, 1944
Size: 801,163 acres
Website: www.nps.gov/bibe

🚗 DISCOVER BIG BEND 🚗

RANGER TIPS

The sun is strong in Big Bend and the weather is unpredictable. Stay hydrated, wear sunscreen and a hat, and bring clothes for different climates.

TAKE IT EASY

Take a leisurely float trip along the Rio Grande through tranquil Boquillas Canyon. A half-day trip lets you explore the park's canyons while kicking back in a raft or heading out on the river in a canoe (right). If you prefer dry land, visit the Rio Grande Village and do some bird-watching. With more than 450 species counted, Big Bend is home to more bird species than any other national park! ⇒

BE EXTREME

"Run" the Rio Grande with a professionally trained white-water-rapid guide (below). Hit Colorado, Contrabando, and Mariscal Canyons—all offering Class 2 and 3 rapids. Check in with the visitor center for details. ⬇

BEST VIEWS

If you're up for a longer hike, head up to South Rim (13 miles round-trip) or Emory Peak (9 miles), two of the highest points in the park providing views of pretty much everything in Big Bend (above). Not up for the trek? Drive to the Rio Grande Overlook to see vistas of the Sierra del Carmen, the river floodplain, and part of a village in Mexico. If you're visiting in the springtime, you'll also get beautiful views of Big Bend's blooming bluebonnets. ⬆

ALL ABOUT ANIMALS

The desert, the mountains, and the river provide habitats for a dizzying array of animals, such as bats, birds (like this scrubjay), snakes, lizards, turtles, fish, mountain lions, and bears. ⬇

385

Persimmon Gap
Visitor Center
4

North

Rosillos

McDonald
Observatory
•Dallas
T E X A S
•Fort Davis
⊙Austin

**BIG BEND
NATIONAL
PARK**

Gulf of
Mexico

0   10 miles

0   10 kilometers

BIG BEND
RANCH
STATE
PARK

118

Terlingua
(Ghost Town)

Study Butte/
Terlingua

118

170

Panther Junction
Visitor Center and
Park Headquarters

CHIHUAHUA
DESERT
NATURE
TRAIL

B I G   B E N D

5

Chisos Basin Campground   Chisos Basin   **4**
Visitor Center
WINDOW VIEW TRAIL
OLD
MAVERICK
ROAD   **3**   ROSS MAXWELL
SCENIC DRIVE

△ *Emory Pk.*
7,825 ft

•Lajitas

N A T I O N A L   P A R

2

Santa Elena
Canyon
Overlook

1

Tuff Canyon   *Chisos Mountains*

*Santa Elena
Canyon*

Rio Grande

Mule Ears Viewpoint

Santa Elena Canyon
River Access

5   Castolon Visitor Center

Cottonwood   **4**
Campground

TEXAS

CHIHUAHUA

RIVER ROAD WEST

U.S.
MEXICO

*Marisca
Can*

Take a Drive

1 Stay in the car and hit the Ross Maxwell Scenic Drive, which winds through the Chihuahuan Desert, past the park's unique rock formations and other highlights, like Mule Ears Viewpoint and Tuff Canyon. Want to venture even further in? Access extremely remote backcountry roads in a guided jeep tour.

2627

D E L   C A R M E N

TEXAS
COAHUILA

Rio Grande Village Visitor Center and Campround

Boquillas Canyon Overlook

o Grande Overlook

4

Boquillas Canyon

RIVER ROAD EAST

5

Rio Grande

Pedal On

3 Big Bend's roads are perfect for pedaling. Mountain bikers have 150 miles of backcountry roads to pick from, while those who prefer smoother journeys can tour the park's 100 miles of paved roads. Either way, you'll have a ride with a view.

Giddy Up

4 Experience the park like a cowboy (or girl): on horseback! Join a saddle horse tour on a trip around old mining towns, by the Rio Grande, and on craggy mountain trails. Ask for details at a visitor center.

[DARE TO EXPLORE]

WALK THROUGH HISTORY

From 1854 to 1891, Fort Davis served as a military post and a place where thousands of emigrants and travelers sought protection prior to the Civil War. Today, you can explore this national historic site and learn more about what life was like way back when. Located in Fort Davis, Texas, about 140 miles from Big Bend. www.nps.gov/foda

PARK HOP

Continue your tour of southwest Texas at Big Bend Ranch State Park, adjacent to the national park. Spy longhorn cattle; hike, bike, or ride a horse on some of the park's 66 miles of trails; or raft along the 23 miles of the Rio Grande managed by Big Bend Ranch. It's also home to Madrid Falls, the second highest waterfall in Texas. www.tpwd.state .tx.us/spdest/findadest/parks/big_bend_ranch

BE A STAR

Love to stargaze? Head to the McDonald Observatory in the Davis Mountains, about 160 miles from Big Bend. Home to the world's largest optical telescopes, the observatory offers you a chance to explore the night sky while learning all about the planets and solar system. www.mcdonaldobservatory.org

MY CHECKLIST

✔ Stop at the park's visitor centers for fun exhibits and important info.

✔ Follow a nature trail and enjoy the surroundings.

✔ Take a ranger-guided hike or a workshop.

✔ Head to Boquillas Canyon for a fun and easy river float.

✔ Explore the park by car—either my own or in a guided jeep tour.

✔ Hike, bike, or travel the park's trails by horseback.

✔ Sleep under the stars at one of the park's campgrounds.

FAST FACT: "Big Bend" refers to the sharp turn the Rio Grande takes in this area.

Welcome to Carlsbad Caverns National Park!

When you enter Carlsbad Caverns National Park

you see acres of rugged terrain, rocky slopes, and wide canyons. What don't you see? The 117 caves carved deep below the Earth's surface, formed millions of years ago. These caverns are open for exploration, where visitors are wowed by giant stalagmites and stalactites, reflective pools, and other funky formations. Above ground, you can camp out and hike among the park's vast deserts and canyons, where many mammals and reptiles roam and cacti stretch their spiny arms to the sky.

State: New Mexico
Established: May 14, 1930
Size: 46,766 acres
Website: www.nps.gov/cave

DISCOVER CARLSBAD CAVERNS

RANGER TIPS

Visit between spring and late fall to see the Mexican free-tailed bats (right) hanging out in the caves. The temperature underground is about 56°F, so make sure to bring a light jacket to stay warm. And stay sturdy on your feet in the caves by wearing comfy shoes with good traction. ↯

TAKE IT EASY

Relax at Rattlesnake Springs picnic area, about 15 miles from the visitor center. Play in the grass or lie under the shade of the large cottonwood trees.

BE EXTREME

Tour Slaughter Canyon Cave for a more "off-road" caving experience and take in the cool formations, such as helictites (below). There is no paved path on this tour, and the only light is from your flashlight. ☻

BEST VIEWS

One of the park's most magnificent views is in the parking area. High above an ancient reef, you can see a striking vista of the ancient seabed and, on a clear day, 100 miles away into Texas.

ALL ABOUT ANIMALS

Besides the abundance of bats, you may also spot mammals like mule deer, mountain lion, black bear, and the Chihuahuan Desert pocket mouse (center), which was not documented in the park until the 21st century. There are also six species of reptiles here, including the gray-banded kingsnake (below), the Rio Grande cooter turtle, and the mottled rock rattlesnake. ↺☻

Go Caving

2 A trip to Carlsbad Caverns (below) is not complete without a look at its caves, which start at 750 feet below the Earth's surface. Hike or take an elevator down to the 8-acre Big Room (where there is a lunch room), then take a guided tour or explore the caverns on your own. Must-see sights? Giant Dome (a 62-foot stalagmite) and the 140-foot-deep Bottomless Pit.

Take a Drive

1 The park's Walnut Canyon drive is a scenic, 7-mile gravel loop that takes you along a ridge to Rattlesnake Canyon, then back to the visitor center through upper Walnut Canyon (right).

0   4 miles

0   4 kilometers

LINCOLN NATIONAL FOREST

Guadalupe Ridge

Rattlesnake Canyon

CARLSBAD

GUADALUPE MOUNTAINS

CAVERNS

Slaughter Canyon Cave

NATIONAL PARK

Rattlesnake Spring Ranger Station

418

Bat Watch

3 From May to October, you can watch 400,000 Mexican free-tailed bats (below) leave Carlsbad Caverns at dusk to feed on insects at the Pecos River. Watch this sensational sight from the park amphitheater (check at the visitor center for the exact time and details).

Bat Flight Amphitheater

Feet below Visitor Center
100 200 300 400 500 600 700 800 900

3 Visitor Center **4** **2** **5**

THE MAIN CORRIDOR

Passage to the Underground Lunchroom and elevators

The Big Room

Feet below Visitor Center
200 300 400 500 600 700 800 900

Giant Dome

Bottomless Pit

Lower Cave

800 900 SCENIC ROOMS

Just For Kids

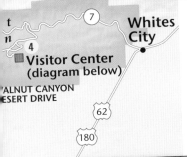

4 Visiting in the summer? Sign up for KidsCorner at the visitor center to learn about bats, caves, plants, and animals of the desert, like the Mexican squirrel (left). You'll also participate in a fun crafts activity or a game.

t
n
7 Whites City
4
■ **Visitor Center** (diagram below)
ALNUT CANYON
ESERT DRIVE

62

180

Santa Fe ⊚
• Albuquerque
NEW MEXICO
Living
Desert
S.P.
Pecos River
White Sands
N.M.
Guadalupe
Mountains N.P.
CARLSBAD CAVERNS NATIONAL PARK
TEXAS

Take a Tour

5 If you opt for a guided tour, consider the Kings Palace tour, a 1.5-hour journey to the deepest portion of the cavern open to the public, 830 feet beneath the desert surface. Look for helictites, draperies, columns (left), and soda straws. Another highlight? The Left Hand Tunnel Tour, a lantern-lit tour highlighting Carlsbad Caverns' history, formations, cave pools, and fossils. Check at the visitor center for details.

[DARE TO EXPLORE]

SMOKEY'S HOME
Back in 1950, a game warden in Lincoln National Forest rescued a black bear cub from a forest fire and named him Smokey Bear—who became the famous symbol of fire prevention. Visit this massive forest, adjacent to Carlsbad Caverns National Park, offering 370 campsites, hiking trails, and plenty of places to picnic. **fs.usda.gov/lincoln**

DUNE IT
Want to see some of the world's largest sand dunes? Check out White Sands National Monument, a whopping 275-square-mile desert about 190 miles from Carlsbad National Park. **www.nps.gov/whsa**

FIND FOSSILS
Go on a fossil hunt in Guadalupe Mountains National Park, featuring a rocky landscape loaded with the bones of prehistoric creatures. **www.nps.gov/gumo**

EXPLORE MORE
Learn about life in the Chihuahuan Desert at Living Desert Zoo State Park, featuring 40 native animal species and hundreds of native cacti and plants. **www.emnrd.state.mn.us/prd/living desert.htm**

MY CHECKLIST
✔ Have a picnic under the cottonwood trees at Rattlesnake Springs.
✔ Stop at the visitor center to learn all about the park.
✔ Take in the park's awesome outside views before heading underground.
✔ Watch Mexican free-tailed bats fly out of caves.
✔ Take a cave tour and check out the cool underground sights.
✔ Enjoy the views from scenic Walnut Canyon Desert Drive.
✔ Experience the lantern-lit tour and check out the Big Room.

FAST FACT: An ancient ocean formed Carlsbad Caverns over 250 million years ago.

Welcome to Grand Canyon National Park!

There really isn't any other way

to describe the massive gorge that serves as the central point of this park other than, well, grand. After all, the mile-deep, 18-mile-wide, 277-mile-long canyon is so big that no matter where you stand, you'll never be able to see it all. But despite the magnet-like draw of the main canyon (nearly five million people visit each year), the three areas of this park also offer trails through cool evergreen forests, a winding river, gurgling streams, cascading waterfalls, and phenomenal views.

State: Arizona
Established: February 26, 1919
Size: 1,217,403 acres
Website: www.nps.gov/grca

DISCOVER GRAND CANYON

RANGER TIPS

Be careful standing near the rim of the canyon, especially when you're trying to get that perfect picture, and carry water at all times—it gets hot!

TAKE IT EASY

Pack a picnic and spread out a blanket at Vista Encantada off of Camp Royal Road. Soak in stunning views of the surrounding park (above) while you snack. ☁

BE EXTREME

Take a river trip through a canyon on the Colorado River (below). Whether you take a day-long tour or one that lasts a week, make sure you're ready for a wet and bumpy ride! Want more adventure? Try Rim Trail, which goes from the canyon's edge for about 13 miles from Pipe Creek Vista to Hermits Rest (a limestone building on the canyon's rim). Note: The path is only paved until you reach Maricopa Point, then it becomes a dirt trail, a part of which is steep. If you get tired, you can always pick up a shuttle bus at any of the main overlooks or at the end of the trail. ☁

BEST VIEW

Check out the Desert View Watchtower, the highest point on the South Rim, featuring views of the Grand Canyon (top), the Painted Desert to the east, and the San Franciso Peaks to the south. Mather Point is another must-see stop, offering a panoramic view into the heart of the Grand Canyon. ☁

ALL ABOUT ANIMALS

Grand Canyon is home to 75 types of mammals, 50 kinds of reptiles and amphibians, 25 species of fish, and more than 300 different birds! Look for bighorn sheep, mule deer, mountain lions, bobcats, coyotes, porcupines, lizards, and frogs. Look up and you'll see hawks, owls, woodpeckers, and perhaps a rare (and endangered) California condor (pictured here). ☁

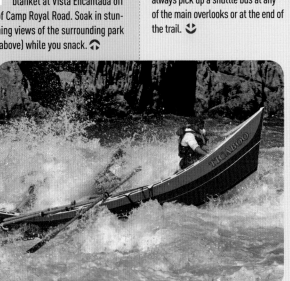

Rock and Roll

1 A visit to the Yavapai Observation Station (below) gets you great views of the canyon, plus a fun lesson in the geology of the area (including a cool carving of the Grand Canyon).

In the Saddle

2 One of the most popular ways to get to the bottom of the canyon is on the back of a mule. Opt for a one-day or overnight trip; if you overnight it, you'll cozy up in a cabin in Phantom Ranch at the bottom of the canyon.

```
0                    10 miles
0          10 kilometers
```

G R A N D   C A N Y O N

N A T I O

K

P

GRAND
CANYON-
PARASHANT
NATIONAL
MONUMENT

5

Colorado River

■ Tuweep
   Ranger
   Station

■ Toroweap Overlook

Grand
Canyon
Skywalk ■

**GRAND CANYON
NATIONAL PARK**

Grand Canyon ■ • Flagstaff
Deer Farm

A R I Z O N A

◎ Phoenix

WEST RIM DRI

Hermi
Re

Ti

Take a Hike

3 Which trails are tops? Try family-friendly Bright Angel Point, Cape Royal, and Cliff Springs Trails—all a mile long or less and offering sensational views of the canyons. Angling for more adventure? Try the 10-mile Widforss Trail for a daylong journey.

Go North

5 The park's less-developed North Rim, 1,000 feet higher than the South Rim, is known as "the road less traveled." Here, you'll find quieter trails through a dense forest—and equally amazing sights throughout the summer (heavy snow keeps this area closed from October to mid-May).

[DARE TO EXPLORE]

RIDE THE RAILS

Board the Grand Canyon Railroad—the only train still servicing a national park—and take a trip into the Old West. Performers will keep you entertained on the 2.5-hour ride with songs, skits, and a reenactment of a cowboy shootout. **www.thetrain.com**

HANDS ON

Feed, pet, and play with deer at the Grand Canyon Deer Farm. You can also see other "residents" like reindeer, wallabies, marmosets, camels, and bison. **www.deerfarm.com**

BRIDGE IN THE SKY

Walk off the edge of a cliff—and onto the Grand Canyon Skywalk, a horseshoe-shaped bridge hanging over the canyon west of the park. Afraid of heights? Don't look down: The bridge, owned by the Hualapai Indian tribe, sits some 4,000 feet above the Colorado River. **www.grandcanyonskywalk.com**

AWESOME ERUPTION

Almost 1,000 years ago, a volcano erupted in an area of what is now Flagstaff, Arizona. Today, the scene at Sunset Crater Volcano National Monument remains eerily preserved: A cinder cone rising 1,000 feet from the ground surrounded by frozen rivers of lava. About 100 miles from Grand Canyon. **www.nps.gov/sucr**

B A B
T E A U

North Rim Entrance Station

Little Colorado River

5 Vista Encantada

DFORSS TRAIL

NORTH RIM

CAPE ROYAL ROAD

3

Bright Angel Point 8,148 ft

CAPE ROYAL TRAIL

Phantom Ranch

2 CLIFF SPRING TRAIL

△ *Cape Royal* 7,865 ft

ricopa Point

Mather Point

Yavapai Point 1

Colorado River

Desert View Watchtower

pot

4

Grand Canyon Visitor Center

SOUTH RIM

GRAND CANYON RAILROAD

180

Tusayan Ruin and Museum

64

MY CHECKLIST

✓ Join the Junior Rangers.

✓ Check out the North Rim area.

✓ Take the park shuttle to all of the main sights.

✓ Explore the South Rim by foot, bus, or car.

✓ Ride a mule to the bottom of the canyon (and back).

✓ Shoot the rapids of the Colorado River.

✓ Shop and stroll in Grand Canyon Village.

Blast From the Past

4 Head to historic Grand Canyon Village, where you'll find buildings dating back to the early 1900s. Stop by the Train Depot and take one of the walking tours. Nearby, you can see the Tusayan Ruin and Museum (left) to get a feel for what life was like for Pueblo Indians 800 years ago.

FAST FACT: The Grand Canyon is one of the Seven Natural Wonders of the World.

⟡ Other Must-see Park Properties in the Southwest

AMISTAD NATIONAL RECREATION AREA (TX)

www.nps.gov/amis

WHY IT'S COOL: It's an oasis in the desert landscape of southern Texas.

WHAT TO DO: Explore prehistoric rock art and a wide variety of plant and animal life; boating, fishing, swimming, and camping.

TRY THIS: Drive across Amistad Dam for a great view and to check out the Mexico–Texas border.

BANDELIER NATIONAL MONUMENT (NM)

www.nps.gov/band

WHY IT'S COOL: The area offers a wild landscape and a unique diversity of habitats that are specific to northern New Mexico.

WHAT TO DO: Tour ancestral Puebloan sites; hiking, picnicking, and backpacking.

TRY THIS: Visiting in the winter? Cross-country ski or snowshoe along the Upper Frijoles Trail (also great for hiking in the warmer months).

BIG THICKET NATIONAL PRESERVE (TX)

www.nps.gov/bith

WHY IT'S COOL: It features an incredible diversity of plants and animals.

WHAT TO DO: Canoeing, rafting, hiking, backpacking, camping, nature walking, and bird-watching.

TRY THIS: Explore the forest by horseback on the Big Sandy Creek Trail.

CANYON DE CHELLY NATIONAL MONUMENT (AZ)

www.nps.gov/cach

WHY IT'S COOL: It's one of the longest continuously inhabited landscapes of North America; it's also home to a modern community of Navajo people.

WHAT TO DO: Tour the canyon and ruins of ancient dwellings; hiking, camping, and horseback riding.

TRY THIS: Take a scenic drive to several overlooks offering amazing views of the canyon.

CHACO CULTURE NATIONAL HISTORICAL PARK (NM)

www.nps.gov/chcu

WHY IT'S COOL: It celebrates the culture of an ancient civilization.

WHAT TO DO: Tour cultural sites and ruins; look for petroglyphs; biking, hiking, and camping.

TRY THIS: Hike to Pueblo Bonito in Chaco Canyon, which was constructed in stages between 850 to 1150 by ancestral Puebloan people.

CHICKASAW NATIONAL RECREATION AREA (OK)

www.nps.gov/chic

WHY IT'S COOL: It's "two parks in one": the Platt Historic District and the Lake of the Arbuckles.

WHAT TO DO: Visit the Travertine Nature Center; boating, camping, hiking, picnicking, biking, bird-watching, swimming, wildlife-watching, and waterskiing.

TRY THIS: Grab your rod and reel and cast a line in the Lake of the Arbuckles, Veterans Lake, and along portions of Rock Creek and Travertine Creek.

CHIRICAHUA NATIONAL MONUMENT (AZ)

www.nps.gov/chir

WHY IT'S COOL: This "Wonderland of Rocks" features stunning rock formations, including pinnacles, columns, spires, and balanced rocks.

WHAT TO DO: Visit Faraway Ranch Historic District, hike, and enjoy scenic drives.

TRY THIS: Up for a challenge? Head to the Heart of Rocks area to see some funky formations like Duck on a Rock, Punch and Judy, and Kissing Rocks.

GILA CLIFF DWELLINGS NATIONAL MONUMENT (NM)

www.nps.gov/gicl

WHY IT'S COOL: It is home to the stone-and-wood cliff dwellings of the Mogollon people, who lived more than 700 years ago.

WHAT TO DO: Take guided tours of the cliff dwellings, hike the Gila and Aldo Leopold Wilderness areas, camp, and visit nearby hot springs.

TRY THIS: Sign up for an archaeological tour of the TJ Site, an unexcavated pueblo usually closed to the public.

GLEN CANYON NATIONAL RECREATION AREA (AZ, UT)

www.nps.gov/glca

WHY IT'S COOL: It offers endless water fun on Lake Powell, the second largest reservoir in the United States.

WHAT TO DO: Waterskiing, swimming, boating, fishing, kayaking, hiking, camping, and bicycling.

TRY THIS: Visit Rainbow Bridge, a national monument and the largest known natural rock arch in the world.

LAKE MEREDITH NATIONAL RECREATION AREA (TX)

www.nps.gov/lamr

WHY IT'S COOL: The lake offers a refreshing spot in the very hot and dry terrain of the Texas Panhandle.

WHAT TO DO: Boating, waterskiing, sailing, scuba diving, fishing, swimming, camping, horseback riding, and hiking in the backcountry.

TRY THIS: Scale to the top of one of the park's scenic overlooks to catch a stunning sunset.

PADRE ISLAND NATIONAL SEASHORE (TX)

www.nps.gov/pais

WHY IT'S COOL: It's the longest undeveloped stretch of barrier island in the world.

WHAT TO DO: Beach-combing, windsurfing, fishing, camping, bicycling, wildlife-watching, hiking, and picnicking.

TRY THIS: Attend a public release of sea turtle hatchlings (check in with the visitor center to find out the times).

SANTA FE NATIONAL HISTORIC TRAIL (CO, KS, MO, NM, OK)

www.nps.gov/safe

WHY IT'S COOL: The trail celebrates the historical significance of this once vital trade route.

WHAT TO DO: Trace the path of the trail using maps and road signs, visit historic sites, and hike trail segments.

TRY THIS: Check out Bent's Old Fort, which served as a supply depot during the Mexican-American War.

Yosemite National Park

Hang gliding over Yosemite National Park offers a panoramic view of some of the West's most stunning wilderness.

the West

the West

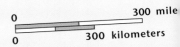

OF ALL OF THE REGIONS in the United States, the West by far has the most national parks. And it's no wonder. Here, you've got it all. You can chill on a tropical island or scale a snow-covered peak. You can hike in the most barren of wildernesses or camp out under a sky sparkling with stars. There are active volcanoes, soaring mountains, majestic glaciers, stunning rock formations, and trees that seem to touch the clouds. Another unique element to the West? The climate is as varied as the landscape: In some locations it's downright cold, like in Mount Rainier in Washington State, while in others it's unbelievably steamy, like in California's Death Valley National Park—the hottest place in North America.

Take a trip to the West and discover large, ancient forests and vast expanses of desert that have been virtually untouched since the days dinosaurs roamed the landscape. Here, you'll find an abundance of animals, from bears to beavers, frogs to foxes, seals to snakes, and almost everything in between. Whatever you do and wherever you roam, one thing's for sure: You will be amazed by the spellbinding sights offered by some of our country's most picturesque parks.

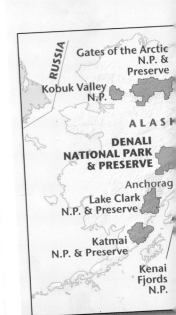

Pacific Ocean

RUSSIA
Gates of the Arctic
N.P. &
Preserve

Kobuk Valley
N.P.

ALASKA

DENALI
NATIONAL PARK
& PRESERVE

Anchorage

Lake Clark
N.P. & Preserve

Katmai
N.P. & Preserve

Kenai
Fjords
N.P.

North Cascades N.P.

CANADA
U.S.

GLACIER NATIONAL PARK

Missouri

Theodore Roosevelt National Park

NORTH DAKOTA

OLYMPIC NATIONAL PARK

• Seattle

WASHINGTON

MOUNT RAINIER NATIONAL PARK

MONTANA

Portland Columbia

• Billings

SOUTH DAKOTA

YELLOWSTONE NATIONAL PARK

OREGON

IDAHO

• Boise

Snake

Badlands National Park

GRAND TETON NATIONAL PARK

Wind Cave National Park

WYOMING

NEBRASKA

Redwood N.P.

Lassen Volcanic N.P.

NEVADA

Salt Lake City

ROCKY MOUNTAIN NATIONAL PARK

• Denver

Crater Lake N.P.

• Reno

Great Basin N.P.

UTAH

Capitol Reef N.P.

Arches N.P.

Colorado

COLORADO

Black Canyon of the Gunnison N.P.

YOSEMITE NATIONAL PARK

BRYCE CANYON NATIONAL PARK

ZION NATIONAL PARK

Canyonlands N.P.

Great Sand Dunes N.P. & Preserve

• San Francisco

Kings Canyon N.P.

Mesa Verde N.P.

Sequoia N.P.

Las Vegas

Grand Canyon National Park

Rio Grande

CALIFORNIA

Death Valley N.P.

• Albuquerque

Channel Islands N.P.

Los Angeles

JOSHUA TREE NATIONAL PARK

Colorado

Petrified Forest N.P.

NEW MEXICO

ARIZONA

TEXAS

San Diego

Saguaro N.P.

Carlsbad Caverns National Park

UNITED STATES
MEXICO

Phoenix

El Paso

Guadalupe Mountains N.P.

Big Bend National Park

CANADA
UNITED STATES

Wrangell-St.Elias N.P. & Preserve

• Juneau

Glacier Bay N.P. & Preserve

HALEAKALĀ NATIONAL PARK

Honolulu

HAWAI'I VOLCANOES NATIONAL PARK

HAWAI'I

400 miles

400 kilometers

0   200 miles

0   200 kilometers

77

Welcome to Bryce Canyon National Park!

Hoodoo *who?* In Bryce Canyon National Park, you'll become instantly familiar with this funny word. Hoodoos, or tall and skinny towers of rock sculpted from snowmelt over thousands of years, are the central point of this park. These fascinating stone pillars attract—and mesmerize—the one million visitors who visit Bryce Canyon each year. But this park's not just about funky formations: There are also plenty of trails to tackle, wildlife to watch, and one of the best views of the night sky you'll get from anywhere on Earth.

State: Utah
Established: September 15, 1928
Size: 35,835 acres
Website: www.nps.gov/brca

DISCOVER BRYCE CANYON

RANGER TIPS

The thin air in the park may make you tired, so take breaks as you need them. You should also wear shoes with good soles and ankle support so you don't slip on the rocky trails.

TAKE IT EASY

If you opt to drive to Rainbow Point, stop for a picnic at the end of the route. Relax in the shadows of fir trees while taking in the sights from the park's highest point (9,115 feet). If you would prefer a simple hike, walk along Queen's Garden Trail (below). 😊

BE EXTREME

Ready to rough it? Set off on the 22.9-mile Under-the-Rim Trail in Bryce's backcountry. Camp under the stars and see the most remote parts of the park. Note: You must have a permit to hike the backcountry. For a different kind of adventure, visit in the winter (right) and try snowshoeing in the park! 😊

BEST VIEWS

Hit the park early to take in the amazing sunrise at Inspiration Point. The glow from the rising sun paints the hoodoos in hues of red, pink, orange, and yellow. For more stunning views, make sure to visit Bryce Point (above), too! 😊

ALL ABOUT ANIMALS

Keep your eyes open for some of Bryce's 59 species of animals, including the endangered Utah prairie dog and the southwestern willow flycatcher. More common creatures? Mule deer (below) and pronghorn. 😊

MY CHECKLIST

✔ Take in the view from Bryce Amphitheater.

✔ Watch the sunrise from Bryce Point.

✔ Get closer to the hoodoos on a walk into a canyon.

✔ Drive to Rainbow Point.

✔ Stay into the evening and stargaze.

✔ Hitch a ride on a horse or mule.

✔ Look out for the endangered Utah prairie dog and other animals.

Camp Out

1 Spend the night under the stars—and under a cover of tall ponderosa pine trees. Choose from two campgrounds within Bryce Canyon National Park. Conveniently, both campgrounds have restrooms, drinking water, and laundry and shower facilities (summer only).

Tropic Reserve

East Fork Sevier River

0 ___ 2 mil

0 ___ 2 kilometer

Natural Bridge Overlook

Pink Cliffs

CANYON

UNDER-THE-RIM TRAIL

BRYCE

Rainbow Point
9,115 ft

2

Salt Lake City

UTAH

Fish Lake National Forest

Red Canyon ■□ **BRYCE CANYON NATIONAL PARK**

Take a Drive

2 Hop on the free park shuttle and hit all of the key sites and viewpoints (summer only). Or stay in your car and drive to Rainbow Point, which climbs more than 1,000 feet—and along awesome overlooks.

GRAND STAIRCASE–ESCALANTE NATIONAL MONUMENT

Stargaze

3 At night, Bryce Canyon offers a breathtaking view of the twinkling sky above. Check out some 7,500 stars visible from Bryce during one of the park's regular Night Sky programs.

Take a Hike

4 Explore the park on one of its 12 trails covering 50 miles and take in the rugged landscape around you. For a great view of the hoodoos hit the 8.6-mile Peek-a-Boo Trail.

COOL CANYON
Check out Red Canyon, home to its own unique red hoodoos, within Dixie National Forest, 9 miles from Bryce Canyon. **www.fs.fed.us/dxnf**

GO FISH
Head to Fishlake National Forest and cast a line in Fish Lake, hopping with trout, including the hybrid splake and the 35-pound Mackinaw. And while you're there, visit the authentic village of the prehistoric Fremont people. About 80 miles from Bryce Canyon. **www.fs.usda.gov/fishlake**

RIDE 'EM, COWBOY
See a real live rodeo at Ruby's Inn, just two minutes from Bryce Canyon's entrance. Every night throughout the summer, you can watch bucking broncos and cool cowboys do their thing in this Old West tradition. **www.rubysinn.com/rodeo**

HOW GRAND
Hop in the car and head to Grand Staircase—Escalante National Monument, a 30-minute drive from Bryce Canyon. Hike to a cascading waterfall, take in the breathtaking sight of Grosvenor Arch, and explore the land where 75-million-year-old dinosaur fossils have been found.
www.ut.blm.gov/monument

amp Canyon
erlook
98 ft

Bryce Canyon Lodge

Sunset Campground

1 **3** Visitor Center

63

North Campground

Sunset Point

NAVAJO LOOP TRAIL

Sunrise Pt.

QUEENS GARDEN TRAIL

5 BRYCE AMPHITHEATER

PEEK-A-BOO LOOP

4

Pink Cliffs

Bryce Point

UNDER-THE-RIM

N A T I O N A L

12

HIGHWAY 12 SCENIC BYWAY

P A R K

12

Tropic

GRAND STAIRCASE-ESCALANTE NAT. MON.

Get in the Saddle

5 Cruise through the canyons on a guided mule or horseback trek in the park. A two-hour trip tours Bryce Amphitheater and lets you see the park's rock formations up close.

FAST FACT: Some hoodoos are taller than a ten-story building!

Welcome to Denali National Park & Preserve!

Spanning an area the size of the state of Massachusetts,

Denali is the home of Mount McKinley, North America's highest peak. And while McKinley (also called Denali) is about as amazing a natural landmark as you can get, it's not all Denali has to offer. Denali is home to a more diverse variety of animals than any other North American park. And when you visit, there's a great chance you'll get to see these amazing creatures, like golden eagles and Dall sheep. But the wildlife that call Denali home are not the only great sights in the park. From its green alpine meadows to its delicate tundra, Denali is packed with scenery unrivaled by any other national park.

State: Alaska
Established: February 26, 1917
Size: 6,075,029 acres
Website: www.nps.gov/dena

DISCOVER DENALI

BEST VIEWS

Soak in spectacular views of Mount McKinley (left) at the Eilson Visitor Center. For great views of some of the other mountains in the park, take a hike on the 3-mile Triple Lakes Trail, where you'll see beautiful views of Mount Fellows, Pyramids Mountain, and other peaks in the Alaska Range. Note: The Triple Lakes Trail is a moderate hike. ↔

RANGER TIPS

Denali is a real wilderness, so be sure to read park safety information before you head out. You should also dress for cool, damp weather—even in the summer. When you hit the road, try to go early for better chances to see wildlife (plus you'll beat the crowds!). And there are no refreshments sold in the park, so bring your own snacks and water.

TAKE IT EASY

Venture to Wonder Lake Campground (below) at mile 85 on the Park Road, the closest campground to Mount McKinley. Picnic and chill as the mountain looms large, just 26 miles away. ↧

BE EXTREME

See Denali from a bird's-eye view on a flight-seeing tour (above). Board a private plane and fly to the tops of the park's peaks, and over its glaciers and lakes. ↥

ALL ABOUT ANIMALS

It would be tough to travel throughout Denali without seeing some of its wildlife. Look for Dall sheep, caribou, moose, wolves, grizzly bears (cub below), black bears, lynx, and over 160 species of birds, like eagles and falcons. ↧

Take a Tour

4 Join an eco-expert for a lesson about Denali's fields, forests, and mountain trails. Biologists, botanists, artists, and authors all offer hands-on programs throughout the year; ask about them at the visitor center.

Bus It

2 Fill your brain with Denali details by taking a bus tour led by a park naturalist. Trips range from a few hours to all day long and take you deep into the park to give you a chance of seeing big game like moose, grizzly bears, and caribou (left).

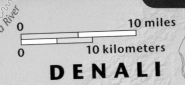

0   10 miles

0   10 kilometers

D E N A L I

Kantishna River

Toklat River

McKinley River

N A T I O N A L

Igloo Cree

Polychrome Overlook

Kantishna.

Toklat River

Wonder Lake

DENALI PARK ROAD

D E N A L I

N A T I O N A L

P R E S E R V E

P A R K

Eielson Visitor Center

1

A N D   P R E S E R V E

R A N G

A

A

L

A

S

K

A

▲ MOUNT McKINLEY
(Denali)
20,320 ft

DENA

STATE

PARK

DENALI

NATIONAL

PRESERVE

Take a Hike

3 Hikes here range from simple strolls to strenuous treks. For a leisurely hike, try the McKinley Station Trail, a 1.5-mile scenic hike through Denali's dense forest. Another highlight? The Horseshoe Lake Trail, which gives you views of the Nenana River.

Majestic Mountain

1 You literally can't miss Mount McKinley (left), the tallest mountain in North America at 20,320 feet. Get a great glimpse of this peak by driving along the 92-mile Denali Park Road, where, on a clear day, you can catch vivid views of the entire mountain. Just be ready for a rugged ride: Only the first 15 miles of the road are paved; the rest is gravel. (Note: Park Road's paved areas are also excellent for biking.)

3

enali Visitor Center
orseshoe Lake Trail)

Healy •

urie Science
Center

5

4

2

nctuary
ver

Park
Headquarters

McKinley
3 Station
Trail

Triple Lakes
Trail

Cantwell

Denali Park
(McKinley Park)

GEORGE
PARKS
HIGHWAY

Nenana River

8

DENALI
HIGHWAY

THE ALASKA RAILROAD

3

Learn More

5 Hit the Murie Science and Learning Center (left), near the Denali Visitor Center, to explore exhibits on Alaska's diverse ecology and collect some cool facts about the 49th state.

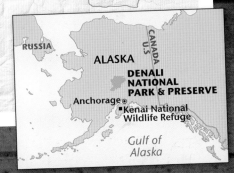

RUSSIA

CANADA
U.S.

ALASKA

DENALI
NATIONAL
PARK & PRESERVE

Anchorage ◉

• Kenai National
Wildlife Refuge

Gulf of Alaska

[DARE TO EXPLORE]

ALL ABOARD
See even more of the amazing Alaska wilderness on the Alaska Railroad. Tour guides point out cool sights easily viewed through the train's large windows as you chug past scenic spots. **www.alaskarailroad.com**

FOR THE DOGS
Meet the amazing huskies that work to patrol the park as part of the Denali ranger team. A tour of the park's kennel offers an inside look at life as a park dog, as rangers share stories about what it's like to "mush." Stop by the visitor center to set up your tour.

FASCINATING FOREST
For more stunning glimpses of Alaska's wildlife and wilderness, visit Chugach National Forest in Anchorage (about four hours from Denali). Stroll along some of the forest's 3,550 miles of coastline, ogle at its glaciers, and spot some of the 200 species of birds that call the Chugach home. **www.fs.usda.us/chugach**

MORE MAMMALS
Marvel at moose, mountain goats, and more at Kenai National Wildlife Refuge, in Soldotna, Alaska. Another animal to watch out for? Furry seals lounging around the refuge's two glacier-carved lakes. **kenai.fws.gov**

MY CHECKLIST

- ✔ Snap some photos of Mount McKinley from various viewpoints.
- ✔ Sign up for a ranger- or naturalist-led program.
- ✔ See the park by bus on a narrated tour.
- ✔ Visit the Murie Science Center.
- ✔ Drive or bike along Park Road.
- ✔ Go flightseeing.
- ✔ Bring binoculars and scope out some wildlife from afar!

FAST FACT: Each year, about a thousand climbers attempt to reach Denali's summit. Only half make it to the top.

Welcome to Glacier National Park!

At the very top of

western Montana you'll find Glacier National Park, a giant swath of land loaded with majestic mountains, turquoise lakes and streams, lush forests, and an array of animals ranging from bears to bald eagles. This area—commonly referred to as the "crown of the continent"—gets its name from the 15,000-year-old glaciers that once could be found almost everywhere you roamed. Time—and sunshine—have altered that view, and now experts say that in less than 25 years, there will be no glaciers left in Glacier National Park.

State: Montana
Established: June 18, 1932
Size: 1,013,572 acres
Website: www.nps.gov/glac

🚗 DISCOVER GLACIER 🚗

RANGER TIPS

Glacier is bear country! To stay safe, read all the suggestions for hiking and camping before you visit, and follow them closely. Keep track of where you are in the park by picking up a trail guide at a visitor center.

TAKE IT EASY

There are a number of beautiful lakes in Glacier National Park (above). Hit the beach at Lake McDonald—the largest lake in the park—where you can boat, swim, fish, or hike along the shore. For an easy stroll head to Avalanche Creek for a self-guided walk through the short Trail of the Cedars. ⌃

BE EXTREME

For an amazing adventure, go on a multiday white-water-rafting trip on the Middle Fork Flathead River (above). Camping and rafting—what's not to love? ⌃

BEST VIEWS

Head to Sun Point via a short nature trail to get a beautiful eyeful of the park's snow-peaked mountains reflecting in the mirror-like surface of St. Mary Lake (below). You can also walk up Avalanche Lake Trail to the glacier-fed Avalanche Lake for wonderful views of the lake, Avalanche Creek, and waterfalls. ⌄

ALL ABOUT ANIMALS

Glacier National Park is home to more than 60 species of mammals and more than 260 species of birds (including the beautiful and colorful harlequin duck). There are about 300 grizzly bears in the park—and plenty of black bears, too. But you're more likely to see mountain goats (below), golden-mantled ground squirrels, bighorn sheep, elk, deer, and moose. There are also a number of gray wolf packs that live in parts of the park. ⌄

87

Map Inset

Map Labels

WATERTON LAKES NATIONAL PARK

6

ALBERTA B.C.

BRITISH COLUMBIA
MONTANA

CANADA
UNITED STATES

ALBERTA
MONTANA

L I V I N G S T O N   R A N G E

Continental Divide

Bowman Lake

Quartz Lake

Many Glacier

Grinnel Glacier

2

FLATHEAD NATIONAL FOREST

North Fork Flathead River

G L A C I E R   R A N G E

Logging Lake

Logan Pass Visitor Center

TRAIL OF CEDARS
NATURE TRAIL
AVALANCHE CREEK TRAIL

5

4

Hidden Lake

Avalanche Lake

N A T I O N A L

Lake McDonald

Mt. Jackson △ 10,052 ft

GOING-TO-THE-SUN ROAD

3

Apgar Visitor Center

West Entrance
Park Headquarters

West Glacier

Belton Railroad Depot

P A R K

Middle Fork Flathead River

2

Big Sky Waterpark

FLATHEAD NATIONAL FOREST

Whitefish

93

Columbia Falls

40

Take a Hike

4 Familiarize yourself with the park's flora and fauna by taking a hike along some of its 700 miles of hiking trails. Highlights include the 3-mile round-trip trail to Hidden Lake (with views of grazing mountain goats and bighorn sheep, flowing waterfalls, and deep glacier valleys along the way).

Go by Boat

5 For a unique view of the park's most pristine spots, hop on an hour-long narrated boat tour. From your vantage point on one of the park's glacier-carved lakes, you'll see glaciers, islands, and waterfalls that are only reachable by boat.

Discovery Zone

3 Check out the Discovery Cabin in Apgar Village to learn about the park's plants and animals, like the bobcat (right). You can also create your own puppet show; sink your hands into a "mystery touch" box; sort rocks, horns, and antlers; and stamp animals into their correct habitats.

Take a Drive

1 Take a scenic drive along the 50-mile Going-to-the-Sun Road, which winds through some of the best sights in northwest Montana. Or park your car for the day and use Glacier's free shuttle (left)—you can hop on and off at any or all of the designated shuttle stops.

Take a Tour

2 Learn from an expert! Join ranger-led walks, talks, and amphitheater programs. Up for a trek? Join a naturalist-led hike and boat ride to the edge of Grinnell Glacier. Check at a park visitor center for the most up-to-date list of offerings.

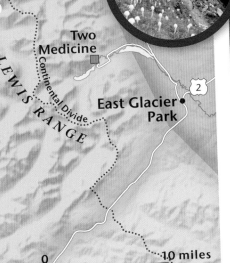

Map labels

89
Babb
Duck Lake
464
Lower St. Mary Lake
Lake Sherburne
Saint Mary Visitor Center
GOING-TO-THE-SUN ROAD
Saint Mary
St. Mary Lake
BLACKFEET INDIAN RESERVATION
1
Two Medicine
LEWIS RANGE
Continental Divide
East Glacier Park
2

0   10 miles
0   10 kilometers

[DARE TO EXPLORE]

HIT THE SHOPS
Stock up on souvenirs at the Glacier Association Bookstore, in the Belton Railroad Depot. Shop for postcards, puzzles, books, games, and more... whatever you think will preserve memories of your time in Glacier. **www.glacierassociation.org**

GO TRIBAL
The town of Browning, Montana—13 miles from Glacier National Park—is home to about 8,000 of the 13,000 people of the Blackfeet Nation, the largest Native American tribe in Montana. Visit the Blackfeet Reservation and tour the Museum of the Plains Indian or the Blackfeet Heritage Center for authentic artwork and crafts. **www.blackfeetnation.com**

SPLASH DOWN
Let loose at the Big Sky Water Park, about 15 miles from Glacier. Take a tube down a giant waterslide, hurl water balloons at your siblings, and have a blast! **www.bigskywp.com**

FUN FOREST
More than 2,000 miles of trails greet you when you reach Flathead National Forest in Kalispell, Montana, about 7 miles from Glacier. Hiking, boating, climbing, fishing, swimming, and horseback riding are some of the many fun options in this forest. **www.fs.usda.gov/flathead**

MY CHECKLIST

✓ Take a drive on Going-to-the-Sun Road.

✓ Ride the park's free shuttle.

✓ Stop by the visitor center to sign up for ranger-led activities.

✓ Check out the Discovery Cabin in Apgar Village.

✓ Chill out at Lake McDonald.

✓ See the sights by boat.

✓ Brave the rapids of the Flathead River.

FAST FACT: Humans first inhabited the Glacier area more than 10,000 years ago.

Welcome to Grand Teton National Park!

The jagged, snow-covered

peaks of the Teton Range—the centerpiece of Grand Teton National Park—are a sight you'll simply never get tired of. The range includes its signature peak, Grand Teton, 13,770 feet (4,198 m) and at least 12 pinnacles over 12,000 feet (3,658 m).

BISON

Occupying a majority of the Jackson Hole valley, the park is not only home to these massive mountains, but also pristine lakes and rivers, and a wide array of wildlife. In the winter, snow bunnies flock to Grand Teton for top-notch cross-country skiing and snowshoe tours. And in the summer, there's nonstop activity, from hiking to horseback riding.

State: Wyoming
Established: February 26, 1929
Size: 309,994 acres
Website: www.nps.gov/grte

DISCOVER GRAND TETON

RANGER TIPS

Always stand at least 300 feet away from large animals like bears, bison, moose, and elk. Taking a hike? Bring water, binoculars, camera, sunscreen, and rain gear.

TAKE IT EASY

Head to the swimming beach at Colter Bay and splash around in the cool, clear water or just relax on the rocky shore. There's also an easy 3-mile nature trail here if you get the itch to hit the woods.

BE EXTREME

Get a true bird's-eye view of the Tetons by paragliding (below)! Along with a professional pilot, you will soar high in the sky. No experience necessary, but you have to weigh at least 40 pounds to paraglide. Afraid of heights? Get your thrills on the water with a rafting trip down the Snake River.

BEST VIEW

Check out a vista of the Tetons, Jackson Lake (left), and Snake River from Signal Mountain. For another great view, take a trip on the Jenny Lake Scenic Drive or visit the Snake River Overlook (above).

ALL ABOUT ANIMALS

Look for mule deer, bison, pronghorn, elk, and moose along the trails. On the water? See if you can spot beavers, herons, swans, badgers, and muskrats. If you're lucky, your eyes just may land on a gray wolf, a coyote (cubs below), a mountain lion, and a grizzly or black bear!

Take the Tram

1 The Aerial Tram (below)—mostly used to transport skiers to the summit of the mountain in the winter—is your ticket to the "Top of the Tetons." Year-round, you can hop off the tram and go on a hike or bird-watching expedition or have lunch at a restaurant perched over 4,000 feet in the sky.

Take a Hike

2 There are more than 200 miles of hiking trails winding around the lakes and through the mountains of Grand Teton. Choose from day hikes (like the always popular Cascade Canyon or Granite Canyon Trails) to multiday backpacking trips. Wherever you go, breathtaking scenery and wildlife sightings are guaranteed!

JOHN D. ROCKEFELLER, JR., MEMORIAL PARKWAY

Yellowstone National Park

GRAND TETON NATIONAL PARK
• Jackson

W Y O M I N G

Cheyenne ◉

G R A N D

JACKSON LAKE

89
191
287

Ranger Peak △ 11,355 ft

Colter Bay Village

Colter Bay Visitor Center

T E T O N

Oxbow Bend Turnout 3

Jackson Lake Dam

Signal Mt. △ 7,727 ft

Mount Moran 12,605 ft △

Leigh Lake

TETON PARK ROAD

3

Snake River

8

N A T I O N A L

4

JENNY LAKE SCENIC DRIVE

191

Inspiration Point

Cascade Canyon

SHUTTLE BOAT

Jenny Lake

Jenny Lake Visitor Center

Grand Teton △ 13,770 ft

P A R K

Teton Science School

TETON PARK ROAD

Craig Thomas Discovery and Visitor Center

• **Moose**

26

Kelly

89
191

Gros Ventre River

Gros Ventre Range

Granite Canyon

13,770 ft

1 AERIAL TRAM

Snake River

NATIONAL ELK REFUGE

5

Teton Village (Jackson Hole Ski Area)

MOOSE-WILSON ROAD

□ **Park Entrance**

To Jackson

2

0 —— 4 miles
0 —— 4 kilometers

Watch for Wildlife

3 Drive the Teton Park Road with your family and keep your eye out for elk, bison (left), and mule deer on the side of the road. Check out the Snake River area to spot bison, moose, and bald eagles. Oxbow Bend is the place for moose, elk, white pelicans, and river otters.

Hit the Water

4 With dozens of lakes dotting the Teton landscape, there is ample opportunity to explore the park by boat. Hop on the passenger boat across Jenny Lake, or canoe or raft on the Snake River (below) or the Jackson Lake Dam. As you paddle, look for wildlife wallowing at the water's edge.

Meet Other Kids

5 From June through September, kids up to eighth grade can hike, play outdoor sports, do science projects (left), and enjoy arts and crafts and water play at Jackson Hole's Kids' Ranch in Teton Village. To learn about ecology and the region's natural history, kids can take a summer course taught by the Teton Science School.

na Matilda Lake

Moran Entrance tation

oran nction 26 287

[DARE TO EXPLORE]

EYE SOME ELK
About 7,000 elk spread out across the 24,700 acres of National Elk Refuge, adjacent to Grand Teton. Visiting in winter? Take a horse-drawn sleigh to see these magnificent animals up close. **www.fs.fws.gov/nationalelkrefuge**

HIT THE TOWN
Spend a day in downtown Jackson, offering family-friendly fun like an alpine slide, mini golf, rodeos, stagecoach rides, souvenir shopping, and more! **www.jacksonholewy.net**

EXPLORE YELLOWSTONE
The famous geysers and spectacular sights of Yellowstone National Park are just a drive away from Grand Teton. Dedicate a day or two to this just-as-awesome park. **www.nps.gov/yell**

GET IN THE SADDLE
Experience the Grand Tetons from the back of a horse! Families can choose from one-hour, two-hour, half-day, and full-day rides. Giddy up! **(800) 628-9988**

MY CHECKLIST

✔ Check out the Craig Thomas Discovery & Visitor Center for park info.

✔ Look for wildlife along the park's trails, roads, and bodies of water.

✔ Join a ranger for a hike, tour, or talk.

✔ Ski, snowshoe, or snowboard if visiting in the winter.

✔ Take a boat or paddle a canoe along Jenny Lake.

✔ Relax and splash at the Colter Bay beach.

✔ Don't miss the view from Inspiration Point.

FAST FACT: The 30-pound trumpeter swan—the largest bird species in North America—can be found in Grand Teton National Park.

Welcome to Haleakala National Park!

Want to see a national park built on a volcano?

Then head to this scenic spot in Maui—Haleakala, a giant dormant volcano forming the eastern side of Hawaii's second-largest island. The big draw to this park (whose name means "house of the sun") is the magnificent Haleakala Crater, stretching 7 miles long and 3 miles deep. Hike around the rim of the crater, take a scenic drive through the park, or just gaze into this natural wonder and dream about the days when lava spewed from this massive mountain.

State: Hawaii
Established: August 1, 1916
Size: 34,294 acres
Website: www.nps.gov/hale

DISCOVER HALEAKALA

BEST VIEW

The view at the Pu'u'ula'ula Summit is just as memorable as the name (which means "red hill"). At an elevation of more than 10,000 feet, you can see the giant volcanoes on the Big Island, plus the neighboring islands of Lanai and Molokai. Sometimes, at night, you can even see the city lights of the island of Oahu to the northwest.

RANGER TIPS

Take two days to explore the park: one on the Haleakala summit (above) and the other in the Kipahulu coastal regions. The summit is windy, damp, and about 30 degrees cooler than the coast, so make sure to pack a jacket! You should also bring your own food and water; neither is sold in Haleakala National Park. ⬆

TAKE IT EASY

Take a relaxing—and refreshing—dip in the cool pools and waterfalls below the highway bridge in 'Ohe'o Gulch (right). Note: This area can be crowded, so keep traveling upstream for a quieter swimming spot. Looking for a great picnic area? Head to Hosmer Grove, located above the park entrance. Beautiful pine and eucalyptus trees surround this shady, cool spot. ➡

BE EXTREME

Take a walk on the wet side with a park naturalist through the Waikamoi Preserve. Be prepared to get muddy as you wind your way 600 feet up a Hawaiian forest (left) on this 5-mile, 5-hour tour. ⬅

ALL ABOUT ANIMALS

Haleakala is one of the very few last sanctuaries for the honeycreeper (below), a tiny, rare native Hawaiian bird. You'll also spot Maui parrotbills, Hawaiian geese, and sea turtles in this environmentally diverse park. ⬇

2 The second part of the park, the Kipahulu Area, is mostly rain forest along Maui's eastern coast. Hike up Pipiwai Trail, which climbs 650 feet through groves of bamboo (left), pools, waterfalls, and cascades.

378

To Kahului

Hosmer Grove

4

5

Park Headquarters Visitor Center

Leleiwi Overlook

WAIKAMOI PRESERVE

0 ——————— 2 miles

0 ——————— 2 kilometers

K a l a p a w i l i   R i d g e

Kalahaku Overlook

Haleakalā Crater

Hanakauhi
8,907 ft

1

HALEAKALĀ NATIONAL

Haleakalā Visitor Center

3

Puʻuʻulaʻula Summit
10,023 ft

Haleakalā
8,201 ft

K a u p ō   G a p

Iao Valley
State Monument

Honolulu

Maui Waiʻanapanapa
State Park

Maui Ocean Center

**HALEAKALĀ
NATIONAL
PARK**

HAWAIʻI

Pacific Ocean

See the Sunrise

3 You really can't beat the amazing sights of Haleakala at daybreak. Rise early and head to the Puʻuʻulaʻula summit for an awesome vantage point. Just remember to dress warmly: Temperatures are often in the 40-degree range at the summit.

Explore the Summit

1 The park's Summit Area—the highest point on Maui—takes you to the Haleakala Crater (right). Here, you can take self-guided hikes or join ranger tours and guided hikes of the area.

[DARE TO EXPLORE]

WAIANAPANAPA NOT?

Explore a cave, fish in the surf, and stroll along the ancient coastal trail in Waianapanapa State Park. About 80 miles from Haleakala National Park. **(808) 984-8109**

JUNGLE FUN

Get lost in the lush Iao Valley State Park, featuring a natural rock pinnacle rising 1,200 feet into the sky. Walk around a botanic garden and splash around in shallow streams and lagoons. About 40 miles from Haleakala National Park. **(808) 984-8109**

FISH FRENZY

Hit the Maui Ocean Center and check out hammerhead sharks, eels, octopi, jellyfish, sea horses, Hawaiian green sea turtles, and a 54-foot-long clear tunnel traveling through a tank of more than 2,000 fish. **www.mauioceancenter.com**

GO DEEP

Board a submarine and sink more than 100 feet below the ocean's surface, where you'll see natural coral reefs, fish, marine life—and a replica of a 19th-century ship creating an awesome artificial reef. **www.atlantisadventures.com**

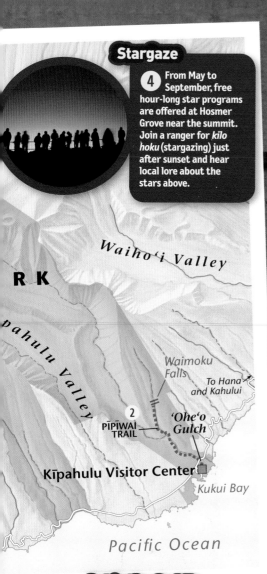

Stargaze

4 From May to September, free hour-long star programs are offered at Hosmer Grove near the summit. Join a ranger for *kilo hoku* (stargazing) just after sunset and hear local lore about the stars above.

Waihoʻi Valley

R K

...pahulu Valley

Waimoku Falls

To Hana and Kahului

2 PĪPĪWAI TRAIL

'Oheʻo Gulch

Kīpahulu Visitor Center

Kukui Bay

Pacific Ocean

Get in the Saddle

5 Private tour groups offer guided horseback rides in Haleakala. Hop in the saddle and enjoy breathtaking sights as you wend through this lush tropical wilderness. Make a trip to the visitor center to find out more about the tours.

MY CHECKLIST

✔ Check out the Haleakala Crater.

✔ Roam through the rain forest valley of Kipahulu.

✔ Hike up to a waterfall.

✔ Go swimming in the cool pools.

✔ Catch a rare glimpse of a honey-creeper bird.

✔ See the sunrise from the summit.

✔ Stay into the evening and stargaze in Hosmer Grove.

FAST FACT: You pass through as many ecological zones on a two-hour drive to the summit of Haleakala as you would on a journey from Mexico to Canada.

Welcome to Hawaii Volcanoes National Park!

Billowing smoke, spewing lava,

and some of the most breathtaking views in the world—that's what you get when you reach Hawaii Volcanoes National Park. Home to two of the world's most active volcanoes, Kīlauea and Mauna Loa, the park stretches from sea level to Mauna Loa's summit some 13,679 feet above the sea.

From the eerie, rugged lava trails of Mauna Loa's wilderness area to the lush, green slopes of Kīlauea, the park is distinguished by its diverse landscape, which makes it a must-see spot on Hawaii's Big Island.

State: Hawaii
Established: August 1, 1916
Size: 333,000 acres
Website: www.nps.gov/havo

DISCOVER HAWAII VOLCANOES

RANGER TIPS

Active volcanoes can be dangerous. Be sure to read the signage carefully. It's also important to stay on marked trails and off of cliffs or steam vents, which can be unstable and slippery.

TAKE IT EASY

Take a breather on the observation deck at the Thomas A. Jaggar Museum. Clear your mind and just take in nature's beauty as you look at the eruptive activity at Halemaʻumaʻu Crater (below). ⬇

BEST VIEW

Head to the Halemaʻumaʻu Overlook, about a ten-minute walk from the Jaggar Museum, for an awesome look into Halemaʻumaʻu Crater (left), which is known as the home of Madame Pele, goddess of Hawaiian volcanoes. The crater is about 3,000 feet across and almost 300 feet deep. ↰

ALL ABOUT ANIMALS

Hawaii Volcanoes is home to critters of all shapes and sizes. Keep your eyes peeled for carnivorous caterpillars, honeycreepers, turtles, hawks, bats, geese, the giant Hawaiian dragonfly (a unique insect with a 5-inch wingspan, making it one of the largest dragonflies in the United States), and the happy-faced spider (pictured here). ⬇

BE EXTREME

Cycle down a volcano! Private tour companies will take you on a downhill adventure from the summit of Kilauea Volcano to the sea (left). On your way down, you'll get to see the volcano up close and personal as you ride through the rain forest and over lava flows. Ask about bike tours at the visitor center. ↰

Cool Tube

3 Take a walk through the Thurston Lava Tube (aka Nahuku, right), formed hundreds of years ago when scalding lava seared a tunnel through a rock. Reach it by taking an easy 15-minute loop trail.

Take a Hike

1 Explore the park on foot! There are plenty of trails through rain forests, deserts, and lava flows. One fun destination? The petroglyphs (below) at Puʻu Loa, a sacred place to the people of Hawaii.

Mauna Loa Weather Observatory

Northeast Rift Zone

HAWAIʻI

△Mauna Loa 13,679 ft

Mauna Loa Lookout

MAUNA LOA ROAD

Southwest Rift Zone

3

Kīlauea
5 Visitor Center

Volca

VOLCANOES

Jaggar Museum **2** Kīlauea Caldera

Halemaʻumaʻu Crater

Overlook

CRATER RIM DRIVE

Chai of Crate

CHAIN OF CRATE ROAD

4

NATIONAL

HILINA PALI ROAD

Hilina Pali Overlook

Hilina Pali

PAR

Southwest Rift Zone

Honolulu

HAWAIʻI

PACIFIC OCEAN

Hawaii

Waikoloa

Mauna Kea Observatory

Akaka Falls S.P.

Kaimu Black Sand Beach

HAWAIʻI VOLCANOES NATIONAL PARK

PACIFIC OCEAN

0 ————— 6 miles
0 ————— 6 kilometers

Learn More

2 Stop by the Thomas A. Jaggar Museum to check out exhibits on volcanoes (including a real seismograph and lava rocks you can touch, left), talk to park rangers, and get a great view of the Kīlauea Caldera and the steaming Halemaʻumaʻu.

Take a Drive

4 Soak in stunning views from your car by traveling two roads that wind through the park. The 11-mile Crater Rim Drive, which includes overlooks (below), loops around Kīlauea Summit and through the lush rain forest; the Chain of Craters Road leads to lava flows and awesome views of impressive craters.

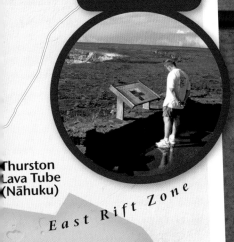

Thurston Lava Tube (Nāhuku)

East Rift Zone

1 ■ Pu'u Loa Petroglyphs

Stay Late

5 After you spend the day exploring, stick around for After Dark in the Park. This program—usually held every Tuesday at 7 p.m. at the Kīlauea Visitor Center Auditorium—features everything from experts speaking about unique elements of the park to live music and entertainment.

[DARE TO EXPLORE]

STAR POWER
Love to stargaze? Head to Mauna Kea, the world's highest island mountain and home of the Mauna Kea Observatory. View the night sky from one of the telescopes, including one that is 16 inches wide! **www.ifa.hawaii.edu/info/vis**

SEE THE FALLS
Head to Akaka Falls State Park to take a walk on a paved path through a green jungle and catch amazing views of the 100-foot cascading Kahuna Falls. About 15 miles from the park. **(808) 974-6200**

FIN FUN
Get in the swim of things by diving into Dolphin Quest, home to a friendly bunch of Atlantic bottlenose dolphins. Pet them, feed them, and watch them flip and leap all around you. In Waikoloa, about 70 miles from the park. **www.dolphinquest.com**

BLACK BEACH
Get a chance to stroll down the newest beach in the world! Kaimu Black Sand Beach in Pahoa dates only to March 2008. Wiggle your toes in the jet-black sand (formed from ground lava rock) as lava flows off Kīlauea in the distance. Across the road from the Kalapana Village Café, about 20 miles from the park.

MY CHECKLIST

✓ Soak in summit views by car or by foot.

✓ Walk through the Thurston Lava Tube.

✓ Peek at the petroglyphs at Pu'u Loa.

✓ Check out the exhibits at the Thomas A. Jaggar Museum.

✓ Ride a bike down the volcano.

✓ Look for lava flows and steam vents.

✓ Join a ranger-led program to find out more about the park.

FAST FACT: Since it began erupting in 1983, Kīlauea has spewed enough lava to make a pathway to the moon and back five times!

Welcome to Joshua Tree National Park!

Joshua Tree may be smack in the middle of a dry desert,

but that doesn't mean it's void of living things. The Joshua tree forest is the largest, tallest, and densest in the United States. And this national park is packed with other plants, too. Colorful ocotillos and desert grasses and wildflowers make this a unique landscape. There are also many animals that call Joshua Tree home (jackrabbits, bighorn sheep, iguanas, and quail are just some of the creatures that may catch your eye). Another fun feature of Joshua Tree? Some of the funkiest rock formations you'll see in North America, plus massive boulders, just perfect for climbing on!

State: California
Established: October 31, 1994
Size: 794,000 acres
Website: www.nps.gov/jotr

DISCOVER JOSHUA TREE

RANGER TIPS

When climbing on the rocks, watch where you put your hands; there are rattlesnakes in Joshua Tree. There are also old mine shafts along some of the hiking trails. Stop and check them out—but never enter a mine.

TAKE IT EASY

Kick back and relax in Cottonwood Spring, a cool, palm-shaded oasis near the southern park entrance. While you relax, make sure to look up. This oasis provides shelter for many bird species, like the rock wren (right). ⮞

BE EXTREME

Go rock climbing (below)! Joshua Tree features more than 400 climbing formations and 8,000 climbing routes. Link up with a guide for important instruction and equipment, then get ready to (literally) scale new heights! ⮟

BEST VIEW

Take the 6-mile trip to Keys View, where you'll score a panoramic view of the Coachella Valley (above), the Salton Sea, and the Sonoran Desert mountains in Mexico. Across the valley you'll see 10,800-foot San Jacinto Peak standing tall over Palm Springs. ⮝

ALL ABOUT ANIMALS

Typical wildlife includes birds (look for roadrunners, mockingbirds, and quail), lizards (like the Chuckwalla, below), toads, and ground squirrels—though you may also spot snakes, bighorn sheep, coyotes, and black-tailed jackrabbits. ⮟

See the "Trees"

1 You can't miss the park's namesake plant, the Joshua tree (right). Learn more about the iconic plant and the rest of the region's diverse desert ecology through displays at the Oasis Visitor Center.

Take a Tour

2 Sign up for a guided tour of the Keys Ranch (below), located in a remote, rocky canyon. Go back in time and glimpse what it took to live and thrive in the Mojave Desert more than 100 years ago.

Joshua Tree Visitor Center
Oasis Visitor Center
247
62
Yucca Valley
PARK BOULEVARD
Wonderland of Rocks
Black Rock Canyon
5
Keys Ranch
J O S H U A
4
Pinto Mountains
Jumbo Rocks
Skull Rock
62
Keys View
Lost Horse Mine
T R E E
PINTO
BASIN
Pinto
Little San Bernardino Mountains
3
Ocotillo Patch
ROAD
10
Cholla Cactus Garden
C o a c h e l l a
V a l l e y
N A T I O N A L

Take a Hike

3 Stroll the self-guided trails through the Cholla Cactus Garden (right) and the Ocotillo Patch, where you can see the Colorado Desert ecosystem up close.

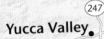

Cottonwood Visitor Center
10
Cottonwood Spring

Rock Stars

4 Make a point to check out Joshua Tree's collection of super-cool rock formations that happen to look a lot like humans, dinosaurs, monsters, cathedrals, or castles. Look for Jumbo Rocks, Skull Rock, and the Wonderland of Rocks.

Camp Out

5 Pitch a tent at the mouth of a canyon at the quiet, family campground at Black Rock Canyon. Sleep under the stars while surrounded by Joshua trees, junipers, cholla cacti, and a variety of desert shrubs.

[DARE TO EXPLORE]

GIANT ROCK

Check out Giant Rock, located just north of Joshua Tree National Park in Landers. At seven stories high and weighing more than 23,000 tons, it's the world's largest solitary boulder. **www.lucernevalley.net/giantrock**

SADDLE UP

Explore Joshua Tree's backcountry by horseback on a guided tour. You'll travel along some of the 253 available miles of equestrian trails and see open lands, canyon bottoms, and dry washes. **www.joshuatreeranch.com**

MORE MOJAVE

Giant sand dunes, volcanic cinder cones, Joshua tree forests, and beautiful wildflowers are all found at the 1.6-million-acre Mojave National Preserve, about a two-hour drive from Joshua Tree. Hint: Run down the "singing" sand dunes to make them go boom! **www.nps.gov/moja**

GO TRIBAL

Collect authentic Indian arrowheads, chase whiptail lizards, and scramble over rocks at Indian Canyons, a preserve that belongs to the Agua Caliente band of Cahuilla Indians. Hike up Murray Canyon, and don't forget your bathing suit—there's a pristine pool under a waterfall for you to cool off in after your climb. About 40 miles from Joshua Tree. **www.indian-canyons.com**

MY CHECKLIST

✔ Start at a visitor center for up-to-the-minute park info.

✔ Meander along a nature trail.

✔ Check out the vistas from Keys View.

✔ Join a guided walking tour of Keys Ranch.

✔ Get active! Mountain climb or bike around the park.

✔ Camp out by a canyon.

✔ See the park's funky rock formations and old mines.

FAST FACT: Joshua trees only grow in the Mojave Desert.

Welcome to Mount Rainier National Park!

Welcoming two million visitors

a year, Mount Rainier is one of the most ecologically diverse national parks in the nation. There are five developed areas in Mount Rainier: Longmire, Paradise, Ohanapecosh, Sunrise, and Carbon/Mowitch. At the center of it all? Mount Rainier, an active volcano that last erupted over a century ago. Surrounding this enormous peak is a magnificent wilderness where you can stroll through blankets of wildflowers, listen for cracking glacier debris, wander through trees more than a thousand years old, and play in the snow all winter long.

State: Washington
Established: March 2, 1899
Size: 235,625 acres
Website: www.nps.gov/mora

DISCOVER MOUNT RAINIER

RANGER TIPS

Mount Rainier is an active volcano! Make sure you check conditions of the mountain before heading out on a hike. And dress for the mountain's unstable weather by carrying extra clothes and rain gear.

TAKE IT EASY

Travel 2,500 feet in ten minutes on the Mount Rainier Gondola (top) to the summit of Crystal Mountain. There, you can eat at the Summit House, the highest restaurant in Washington State. ⛰

BE EXTREME

Rent a bike (below) and hit the park's pipeline trail. Follow this mostly flat, dirt road until you hit Packwood Lake, where you can soak up the views of Rainier and the Goat Rocks Wilderness. If you're in the mood for an exciting hike, head to the Carbon River at the park's northwest corner entrance. Here you can check out a rain forest and hike to a dark, shiny glacier. Note: Check for road closures before you head out. ⬇

BEST VIEW

Head to the Sunrise Visitor Center (left) for some of the most amazing sights in the park. From 6,400 feet above sea level, you'll take in views of Mount Rainier, Emmons Glacier, and other volcanoes in the Cascade Range. ⬅

ALL ABOUT ANIMALS

The diverse landscape of Mount Rainier provides habitats for all kinds of animals, such as elk, deer, goats, black bears, marmots, birds (like the Clark's nutcracker, below), fish, and frogs. Invertebrates are the most abundant, making up 85 percent of all animals in the park. ⬇

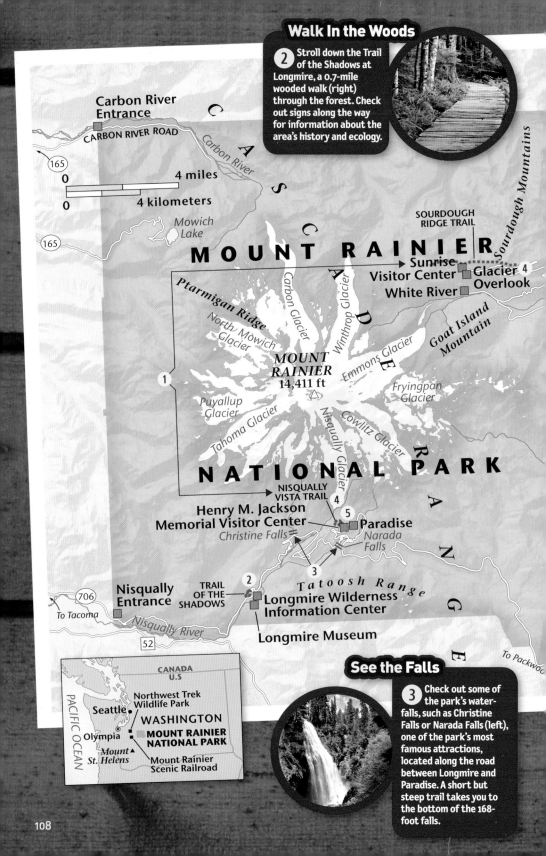

2 Stroll down the Trail of the Shadows at Longmire, a 0.7-mile wooded walk (right) through the forest. Check out signs along the way for information about the area's history and ecology.

Carbon River Entrance

CARBON RIVER ROAD

Carbon River

165

0   4 miles

0   4 kilometers

165

Mowich Lake

SOURDOUGH RIDGE TRAIL

MOUNT RAINIER

Sourdough Mountains

Sunrise Visitor Center

Glacier Overlook **4**

White River

Ptarmigan Ridge

Carbon Glacier

Winthrop Glacier

North Mowich Glacier

Goat Island Mountain

Emmons Glacier

1

MOUNT RAINIER 14,411 ft

Fryingpan Glacier

Puyallup Glacier

Tahoma Glacier

Nisqually Glacier

Cowlitz Glacier

NATIONAL PARK

NISQUALLY VISTA TRAIL

Henry M. Jackson Memorial Visitor Center

Christine Falls

4

5 Paradise

Narada Falls

3

Nisqually Entrance

TRAIL OF THE SHADOWS

2

T a t o o s h   R a n g e

Longmire Wilderness Information Center

706

To Tacoma

Nisqually River

Longmire Museum

52

RANGE

To Packwood

CANADA
U.S

Northwest Trek Wildlife Park

PACIFIC OCEAN

Seattle

WASHINGTON

Olympia

MOUNT RAINIER NATIONAL PARK

Mount St. Helens

Mount Rainier Scenic Railroad

3 Check out some of the park's waterfalls, such as Christine Falls or Narada Falls (left), one of the park's most famous attractions, located along the road between Longmire and Paradise. A short but steep trail takes you to the bottom of the 168-foot falls.

Take a Hike

1 The park has huge hike potential—260 miles of maintained trails, to be exact. Check out the Nisqually Vista Trail, a 1.2-mile loop trail with great views of Mount Rainier. Or head to the Sunrise Visitor Center to find trailheads for hikes like the Sourdough Ridge Trail, offering sights of Mount Rainier, glaciers, and other volcanoes in the Cascade Range.

Sunrise Mountain
Crystal Mountain
Sunrise Ridge
White River
GONDOLA
Crystal Mountain Ski Resort

White River Entrance

MATHER MEMORIAL PARKWAY   To Yakima

410

123

Ohanapecosh River

Stevens Canyon Entrance

Ohanapecosh Visitor Center

Great Glacier

4 Head to Nisqually Glacier (below), the best known of the park's 26 glaciers. Get there by walking about a mile from the Glacier View Overlook (on the road that leads from Nisqually to Paradise).

Snow Cool

5 Visiting in the winter? Hit the Paradise area for all sorts of "cool" fun. Park rangers lead guided snowshoe walks on weekends from late December through early April (leaving from the Henry M. Jackson Memorial Visitor Center at Paradise). You can also go snowboarding, skiing, and tubing when there's sufficient snow.

[DARE TO EXPLORE]

GO TO GIFFORD
Snag spectacular views of Mount St. Helens from Gifford Pinchot National Forest, about 10 miles from Mount Rainier National Park. You can also see glaciers and a variety of plants and animals spread across seven wilderness areas. **www.fs.usda.gov/giffordpinchot**

RAD REGROWTH
The 1980 eruption of Mount St. Helen's destroyed every living thing around it. Today, a beautiful forest has emerged from the once charred land, which you can explore at Mount St. Helens National Volcanic Monument, located within Gifford Pinchot National Forest. **www.fs.usda.gov/mountsthelens**

ALL ABOARD
Take a scenic ride through the countryside aboard the Mount Rainier Scenic Railroad, a vintage logging locomotive. Listen as the conductor offers a history lesson of the breathtaking sights you pass on the 18-mile journey. **www.mrsr.com**

WILDLIFE GALORE
You're guaranteed to see some cool animals at the Northwest Trek Wildlife Park near Eatonville, Washington (about 25 miles from the park). Search for wildlife like bears, bison, wolves, owls, and more as you wander through forests, wetlands, and meadows on the park's tram. **www.nwtrek.org**

MY CHECKLIST

- ✔ TAKE A GLIMPSE AT A GLACIER.
- ✔ WALK TO A WATERFALL.
- ✔ HIT THE TRAILS OR TAKE IN A NATURE WALK.
- ✔ RIDE THE GONDOLA TO THE SUMMIT OF CRYSTAL MOUNTAIN.
- ✔ PLAY IN PARADISE'S SNOW PARK DURING THE WINTER.
- ✔ EARN A JUNIOR RANGER BADGE.
- ✔ RIDE A BIKE ALONG THE PARK'S PIPELINE TRAIL.

FAST FACT: There are 26 glaciers, 392 lakes, and 470 rivers and streams in Mount Rainier.

ORCA

Welcome to Olympic National Park!

Warmly referred to as "a gift from the sea,"

Olympic National Park preserves more than 60 miles of Washington State coastal wilderness. The park features three major ecosystems (subalpine, coastal, and forest), which include emerald green rain forests, rocky strips of coastline, natural hot springs, more than 3,000 miles of rivers and streams, and some of the world's oldest trees. Olympic is also home to many different animals, including 37 species of native fish. It's no wonder that more than three million people visit this spot every year, making it one of the country's most popular national parks.

State: Washington
Established: June 29, 1938
Size: 922,000 acres
Website: www.nps.gov/olym

DISCOVER OLYMPIC

RANGER TIPS

This park is huge! Ask a ranger for recommendations on things to do based on how much time you have to explore the park. When traveling along the coast, know the tides; bring a map and tide chart to plan your route. And make sure to bring rain gear and layer up—weather around Olympic is unpredictable.

BEST VIEW

Climb to Hurricane Ridge (above), where you'll see the awesome Olympic Mountains (even more amazing at sunset). While you're up there, look for the rare Olympic marmot! ⌂

ALL ABOUT ANIMALS

Elk, elk, and more elk (below)! Olympic is home to the largest unmanaged herd of Roosevelt elk in the world. You may also see mountain goats, pikas, squirrels, lynx, foxes, coyotes, wolverines, grizzly bears, bighorn sheep, and about 300 species of birds. On the water? Watch for dolphins, whales, sea lions, seals, and sea otters. ☮

TAKE IT EASY

Chill out at Rialto Beach (above). Collect driftwood on its rocky shores, climb on giant logs, and take in views of the park's iconic seastacks (rock formations in the water). If you're up for a short hike, walk 1.5 miles north to see Hole-in-the-Wall, a stunning sea-carved arch. ⌂

BE EXTREME

Ride the rapids (below)! A guide will take you on an exciting course down the Elwha River, the Hoh River, or straight through the heart of the Hoh Rain Forest. Whatever water you hit, get ready for a *splash*-tastic time! If you're visiting in the winter, go sledding at Hurricane Ridge. Note: Check weather conditions and park closure information before you go. ☮

CANADA
U.S.

OLYMPIC NATIONAL PARK

PACIFIC OCEAN

Seattle
WASHINGTON
Olympia

Go Green

1 You won't want to miss the amazing array of flora and fauna in the Hoh Rain Forest (right). An average of 134 inches of rain falls here every year, allowing ferns, moss, and the 1,000-year-old Sitka spruce trees to thrive. Get there via the Hall of Mosses Trail, which you access at the Hoh Rain Forest Visitor Center.

CANADA
U.S.

Strait of Ju

PACIFIC OCEAN

OZETTE LOOP TRAIL
Ozette
HOKO-OZETTE ROAD

113

2

Storm King Information Station

112

Ozette Lake

Sappho

101

Sol Duc River

Fairholm

3 Lake Crescent

Marymere Falls

4

Eagle

Hole-in-the-Wall

110

Forks
USFS/NPS Information Station

Sol Duc Falls

O L Y

Rialto Beach
La Push

Mora

110

Bogachiel River

101

Hoh Rain Forest Visitor Center

1

Mount Olympus 7,965 ft.

UPPER HOH ROAD

Hoh River

N A

O

L

0   10 miles

0   10 kilometers

Take a Hike

2 Explore some of the park's hundreds of trails, observation points, and vistas. Highlights include the Hurricane Ridge area (to see peaks and glaciers in the distance) and the Ozette Loop Trail along the park's sandy, rocky coast. While on the coast you may even spot a sea lion (below)!

Clearwater River

M O

Queets River

Kalaloch Information Station

Queets

Quinault Rain Forest Ranger Station

NORTH SHORE ROAD

101

Quinault Information Station

Quinaul Lake

Paddle On

3 Go kayaking, canoeing, or sailing on the glacially carved Lake Crescent (left), tucked in the northern foothills of the Olympic Mountains. Crescent's clear waters allow you to see 60 feet down to the bottom!

Follow the Falls

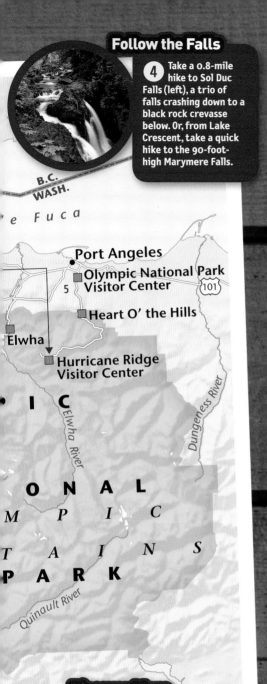

4 Take a 0.8-mile hike to Sol Duc Falls (left), a trio of falls crashing down to a black rock crevasse below. Or, from Lake Crescent, take a quick hike to the 90-foot-high Marymere Falls.

B.C.
WASH.

e F u c a

Port Angeles
Olympic National Park
Visitor Center
5
101
Heart O' the Hills
Elwha
Hurricane Ridge
Visitor Center

Dungeness River

Elwha River

I C

O N A L

M P I C

T A I N S

P A R K

Quinault River

Discover More

5 Dress up like a park ranger, play games, and get hands on with artifacts like deer antlers and animal fur at the Children's Discovery Room at the Olympic National Park Visitor Center.

PARK RANGER

[DARE TO EXPLORE]

DISCOVER MORE
Visit the Olympic Coast Discovery Center to learn more about marine wildlife in the area. It's also a great spot to search for whales out in the water. **www.olympiccoast.noaa.gov/AboutUs**

GO ON SAFARI
Take a safari through Olympic's Quinalt Rain Forest. From the comforts of a bus, you can see huge (and ancient!) trees and wildlife, and learn fun facts provided by knowledgeable guides. **www. beelinetours.com/creative_olympicgroup.html**

TWILIGHT TOUR
"Twihards" flock to Forks, the town featured in the Twilight book series by Stephenie Meyer. Pick up a packet at the Forks Chamber of Commerce visitor center for a map that will take you to some of the most memorable sites from the books. About 100 miles from Olympic National Park. **www.forkswa.com**

AMAZING ANIMALS
Get up close and personal with wildlife at the Olympic Game Farm, originally a home for animal actors featured in Disney movies back in the 1960s. Today, the farm is open to the public and features a bevy of animals, from lions to llamas. **www.olygamefarm.com**

MY CHECKLIST

✔ VISIT THE HOH RAIN FOREST.

✔ HIKE TO HURRICANE RIDGE.

✔ RIDE THE RAPIDS OF THE ELWHA OR HOH RIVERS.

✔ STROLL THE ROCKY COAST AND SEE A SEASTACK.

✔ GAWK AT MUST-SEE TREES, LIKE THE SITKA SPRUCE.

✔ PADDLE ALONG LAKE CRESCENT.

✔ HAVE MORE FUN AT THE CHILDREN'S DISCOVERY CENTER!

FAST FACT: Winds at Hurricane Ridge can blow up to 75 miles an hour!

Welcome to Rocky Mountain National Park!

Lift your senses to a new level in

Rocky Mountain National Park. With elevations ranging from 8,000 feet to 14,259 feet, you'll see all sorts of amazing sights, from jagged snowcapped mountains to colorful blooms of wildflowers to pristine lakes. Just under 80 miles from Denver, this park features 359 miles of hiking trails, each offering an amazing, up-close-and-personal peek at wetlands, forests, and tundra.

Whether you visit in the winter, spring, summer, or fall, you're bound to be wowed by the Rockies.

State: Colorado
Established: January 26, 1915
Size: 265,873 acres
Website: www.nps.gov/romo

DISCOVER ROCKY MOUNTAINS

RANGER TIPS

Take your time and drink plenty of water. The Rockies' thin air may tire you out and dehydrate you more quickly than normal. You should also layer up! The weather in the Rockies shifts drastically during the day, so be prepared for both hot and cold temperatures. And be aware of your surroundings: Mountain lion and black bear sightings have increased over the past several years.

BEST VIEW

Head to the Alpine Visitor Center, located 11,798 feet above sea level, for unrivaled glimpses at ancient glacial valleys, alpine tundra (right), and Fall River. You can also head to Sprague Lake to take an easy half-mile nature walk where you will be surrounded by amazing views of the magical mountain peaks of the Continental Divide. ⇢

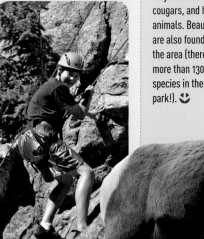

TAKE IT EASY

Go for a picnic! The park has many opportunities for picnicking, both on the east side and the west side of the park. Popular spots are Sprague Lake on the east and Coyote Valley on the west. Dream Lake (above) is also a great place to fish and enjoy the view. ⬆

BE EXTREME

Take a rock-climbing course (right) with the Colorado Mountain School, an organization authorized to teach kids how to climb in the park. ⇢

ALL ABOUT ANIMALS

The park is famous for its large animals, like elk, bighorn sheep (below), moose, and mule deer. You may also see coyotes, black bears, cougars, and hundreds of smaller animals. Beautiful butterflies are also found all over the area (there are more than 130 species in the park!). ⬇

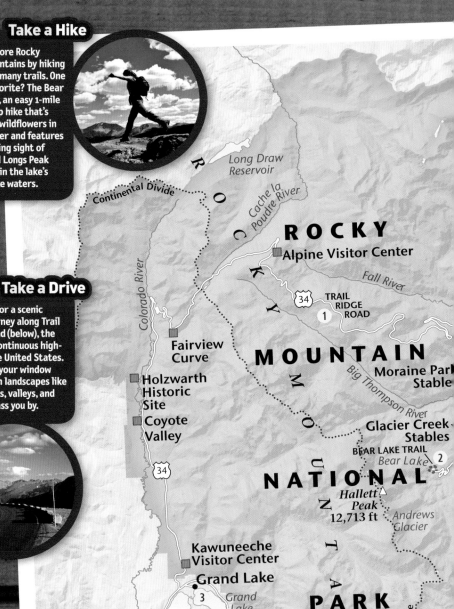

Take a Hike

2 Explore Rocky Mountains by hiking one of its many trails. One family favorite? The Bear Lake Trail, an easy 1-mile round-trip hike that's ripe with wildflowers in the summer and features the stunning sight of Hallet and Longs Peak reflected in the lake's mirror-like waters.

Take a Drive

1 Go for a scenic journey along Trail Ridge Road (below), the highest continuous highway in the United States. Look out your window and watch landscapes like mountains, valleys, and tundra pass you by.

Snow Fun

3 Hitting the park in the winter? Go snowshoeing or sledding! (Just make sure your parents inspect an area to ensure it is safe for you to play.) There's also Grand Lake's Winter Carnival every year, featuring snowmobile events, snow sculpture contests, and more.

Long Draw Reservoir

Cache la Poudre River

Continental Divide

R O C K Y

Alpine Visitor Center

Fall River

34 TRAIL RIDGE ROAD **1**

Colorado River

M O U N T A I N

Fairview Curve

Moraine Park Stable

Big Thompson River

Holzwarth Historic Site

Coyote Valley

Glacier Creek Stables

BEAR LAKE TRAIL

Bear Lake **2**

34

N A T I O N A L

Hallett Peak 12,713 ft

Andrews Glacier

Kawuneeche Visitor Center

Grand Lake

3

Grand Lake

P A R K

Continental Divide

Shadow Mountain Lake

Colorado River

0   4 miles
0   4 kilometers

Lake Granby

ROCKY MOUNTAIN NATIONAL PARK

°Denver

Florissant Fossil Beds
National Monument■

COLORADO

Beaver
Meadows
Visitor Center

Fall River
Visitor
Center

Big
Thompson
River

34

Estes
Park

34

36 · 4

5

Moraine Park
Visitor Center

7

BEAR
LAKE
ROAD

5

Sprague L.

SPRAGUE
LAKE NATURE
TRAIL

Lily Lake
Visitor Center

Longs
Peak

ongs Peak
4,259 ft

Meeker
Park

Discover More

4 Handle cool arti-
facts like animal
skins and skulls at the
Beaver Meadows Visitor
Center (below). While
you're there, join a
25-minute ranger talk
on the local wildlife and
history of the Rockies.

Get in the Saddle

5 Soak in the scenery
while riding a horse!
Hit the hundreds of miles
of horse trails and get the
perfect vantage point for
wildlife-watching and
sightseeing.

[DARE TO EXPLORE]

FOSSIL FUN
Visit the most diverse fossil deposits in the world
at Florissant Fossil Beds National Monument.
Explore 14-foot-wide petrified redwoods and thousands of detailed insect and plant fossils. About
160 miles from the Rockies. **www.nps.gov/flfo**

SWEET RIDE
Head to Ride-a-Kart in nearby Estes Park and
have some fun! Challenge your siblings to a go-
kart race, hit a homer in the batting cage, and
flip out on the bungee trampoline.
www.rideakart.com

COWBOY SONG
Get a taste for the Old West at a cowboy sing-
along! Local musicians perform folk songs
around a campfire throughout the summer in
downtown Estes Park. Call ahead to find out the
dates and times. **(800) 44-ESTES**

COOL, DUDE
Hit the Holzwarth Historic Site within the park.
Here, you'll find a fully restored dude ranch from
the 1920s. Take a tour to see what life was like
back then with a guided tour of the property—
and a look at the furniture, tools, and other features that welcomed mountain travelers to this
spot almost 100 years ago. **(970) 586-1206**

MY CHECKLIST

✔ Take a drive on Trail Ridge Road.

✔ Horseback ride through the park.

✔ Check out the sights from the
Alpine Visitor Center.

✔ Chat with a ranger at Beaver
Meadow.

✔ Raft down the Colorado River.

✔ Snowshoe and sled in the winter.

✔ Become a Junior Ranger!

FAST FACT: Rocky Mountain National Park is
open 24 hours a day, 365 days a year.

Welcome to Yellowstone National Park!

Arguably the most famous park

in the world, Yellowstone is also the oldest. Established in 1872, Yellowstone falls within three states (Wyoming, Montana, and Idaho) and is bigger than Rhode Island and Delaware combined! Another amazing fact about Yellowstone? There are more geysers and hot springs here than anywhere else on Earth. And it's those gushing geysers combined with the park's vivid views (not to mention wildlife galore!) that make Yellowstone a must-see destination for any fan of the great outdoors.

States: Idaho, Montana, Wyoming
Established: March 1, 1872
Size: 2,221,766 acres
Website: www.nps.gov/yell

DISCOVER YELLOWSTONE

RANGER TIPS

Stay at least 25 yards away from bison or elk and 100 yards away from bears (it's the law). Ask a ranger about geyser schedules so you don't miss an amazing eruption! And make sure to keep your distance from the boiling water of the thermal pools.

TAKE IT EASY

Up for a swim? Head to the swimming hole near Firehole Falls. At a spot where the warm thermal waters mix with the freezing mountain runoff, the temperature is about as perfect as you can get. For a relaxing boat ride, make your way to the Bridge Bay Marina (below), where you can take a boat out to do some sightseeing.

BE EXTREME

Take a soak in the hot spring stream where the Boiling River meets the Gardner River (top left). (Don't worry, the water isn't actually boiling—it's quite comfortable—but make sure to stay in designated soaking spots!)

BEST VIEW

Head out on Canyon Rim Drive to check out great views of the Grand Canyon of Yellowstone and the Yellowstone River's Lower Falls (left). This waterfall is 308 feet high—that's almost twice the height of Niagara Falls!

ALL ABOUT ANIMALS

Yellowstone is spilling over with wildlife such as elk, wolves (below), moose, bison, bighorn sheep, coyotes, mountain lions, trumpeter swans, grizzly bears, and 311 species of birds. Head to Lamar Valley or Hayden Valley to see some of these animals grazing in the grass. To increase the chance of sighting wildlife, it's best to hit these areas early in the morning or in the evening.

Smelly Springs

1 What's that smell? It's just Mammoth Hot Springs, which emits a rotten egg stench, thanks to the sulfur in the water. If you don't mind the aroma, there's plenty to do here: check out natural pools, see Minerva Terrace (below), and visit the Albright Visitor Center & Museum for a park history lesson.

Great Geysers

2 Head to the park's Upper Geyser Basin to see the iconic Old Faithful Geyser, which erupts every 45 to 110 minutes. From there, follow the path to Castle Geyser (known for the tall cone built around the vent, below) and Morning Glory Pool, named for its deep, aqua waters.

Buffalo Bill Historical Center

YELLOWSTONE NATIONAL PARK

Grand Teton National Park

Wyoming Dinosaur Center

W Y O M I N G

Cheyenne ●

89

Gardiner

North Entrance
Mammoth Hot Springs
Minerva Terrace

5 45th Parallel Bridge

MONTANA
WYOMING

1

Albright Visitor Center

Yellowstone River

Boiling River

Gardner River

GALLATIN RANGE

Roosevelt Corrals

191

Y E L L O W S T O N E

GRAND LOOP ROAD

191

287

Norris Museum ● Norris

NORTH RIM DRIVE

4 Grand Canyon of the Yellowstone

20

West Yellowstone

89

NORTH RIM TRAIL

Lower Falls

SOUTH RIM DRIVE

Canyon Village Visitor Center

West Entrance

Madison

Firehole Falls

Firehole River

N A T I O N A L

GRAND LOOP ROAD

3 FIREHOLE LAKE DRIVE

Great Fountain Geyser

Fishing Bridge Visitor Center

Castle Geyser

Upper Geyser Basin

2

Old Faithful Geyser

Bridge Bay Marina

Visitor Center

Yellowstone Lake

WYOMING
IDAHO

Morning Glory Pool

Sheshone Lake

Grant Village Visitor Center

P A R K

Lewis Lake

Heart Lake

Mount Sheridan 10,305 ft

Continental Divide

89

191

Snake River

287

South Entrance

JOHN D. ROCKEFELLER, JR., MEMORIAL PARKWAY

0   10 miles

0   10 kilometers

GRAND TETON N.P.

Line It Up

5 Head to the 45th Parallel Bridge, a famed photo-op spot at the border of Montana and Wyoming within the park. Visitors snap shots in front of a sign marking an imaginary line that circles the globe halfway between the Equator and the North Pole (below).

Silver Gate

212

Northeast Entrance

45th Parallel
HALF WAY BETWEEN
THE EQUATOR AND
NORTH POLE

A B S A R O K A   R A N G E

Cool Canyon

4 Yellowstone boasts its own Grand Canyon, a 900-foot-deep and half-mile-wide rocky hole that's definitely a sight to see (below). Head to Canyon Village and the Canyon Rim Trail for an up-close view. While you're here, check out the Canyon Visitor Center for fun exhibits.

East Entrance

16   20

14

△ Eagle Peak
11,367 ft

Yellowstone River

Take a Drive

3 Many of Yellowstone's famous sights can be seen from the road. One memorable ride? The Firehole Lake Drive, which offers viewpoints of thermal features like the Great Fountain Geyser, which sometimes shoots steam and water up to 200 feet in the air!

[DARE TO EXPLORE]

GRAND ADVENTURE
While you're in Wyoming, you won't want to miss Grand Teton National Park. Go for hikes, hang out at the Kids Ranch, walk around downtown Jackson Hole, and just soak in the sights of the park's magnificent mountain range. **www.nps.gov/grte**

DINO-MITE
Rated the number one dinosaur museum in the country, Wyoming Dinosaur Center is a must-see for paleontology buffs. See over 30 mounted skeletons of dinosaurs, check out a dinosaur dig site, and more. About 30 minutes from Yellowstone National Park. **www.wyodino.org**

ON THE WAGON
Jump into the Wild West with a stagecoach adventure and cookout! Take a ride on a horse-drawn covered wagon, eat some steak prepared by real cowboys, and look for wildlife during a rustic 45-minute ride that leaves from the Roosevelt Corral in Yellowstone. **(866) 439-7375**

HISTORY LESSON
Go back in time at the Buffalo Bill Historical Center. Learn about the American West, Yellowstone natural history, and famous cowboy Buffalo Bill Cody in this museum, located about 100 miles from Yellowstone. **www.bbhc.org**

MY CHECKLIST

✔ Hike around Yellowstone Canyon.

✔ Ogle at Old Faithful and other geysers.

✔ Snap some pics at the 45th Parallel Bridge.

✔ Go swimming near Firehole Falls.

✔ Check out exhibits at Yellowstone's museums and visitor centers.

✔ Smell the unusual aroma of Mammoth Hot Springs.

✔ Keep eyes peeled for animals like bears, elk, and bighorn sheep.

FAST FACT: The Green Dragon Geyser gets its name from the boiling green water it shoots into the sky.

YOSEMITE NATIONAL PARK, CALIFORNIA

Welcome to Yosemite National Park!

Spanning almost 800,000 acres in east-central California, this park is roughly the size of Rhode Island. Here, towering trees reach toward the sky, their images reflected in the mirrored lakes below, while waterfalls splash into deep valleys. Majestic mountains, covered with colorful wildflowers and a variety of vegetation, are home to an amazing array of wildlife such as the American black bear, spotted owl, mountain lion, and mule deer. Wherever you roam, you'll be blown away by nature's breathtaking beauty. It's no wonder that Yosemite is one of the most popular parks on the planet. From horseback riding to hiking, one thing's for sure: You'll never be bored here!

State: California
Established: October 1, 1890
Size: 761,266 acres
Website: www.nps.gov/yose

DISCOVER YOSEMITE

RANGER TIPS

To beat the crowds, avoid visiting on a holiday weekend, and hit the hiking trails first thing in the morning. Keep your distance from the mule deer, which often come close to humans.

TAKE IT EASY

Take a break from the action by lounging at Sentinel Beach, a wide and sandy picnic area on the Merced River (Cathedral Beach is also a quiet spot). Or hit up the outdoor swimming pool in Curry Village. If you would rather soak under a waterfall (right), you can do that, too. ➷

BEST VIEWS

Bring your camera to Tunnel View Overlook, said to be the most photographed vista on Earth. Up for a challenge? Take a 3.6-mile hike to Upper Yosemite Fall and be rewarded with spectacular valley views. Then, at dusk, head to Half Dome (below), where the setting sun casts a gentle glow throughout the eastern end of Yosemite Valley. ☽

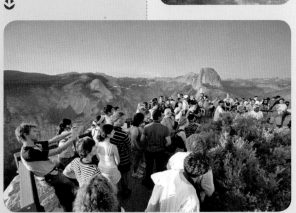

BE EXTREME

A magnet for thrill seekers, Yosemite offers one exciting adventure after the next. Within the park you can hang glide off Glacier Point, float down the Merced River in a raft, and rock climb up the famous nose of El Capitan (above). ⌂

ANIMAL SIGHTINGS

A trip to Yosemite just won't be complete without a glimpse of golden-mantled ground squirrels. These chipmunk look-alikes mostly live by the giant sequoia grove. Also watch for Steller's jays (the loudest birds in Yosemite), mule deer, rabbits, coyotes, and maybe even a black bear (pictured here). ☽

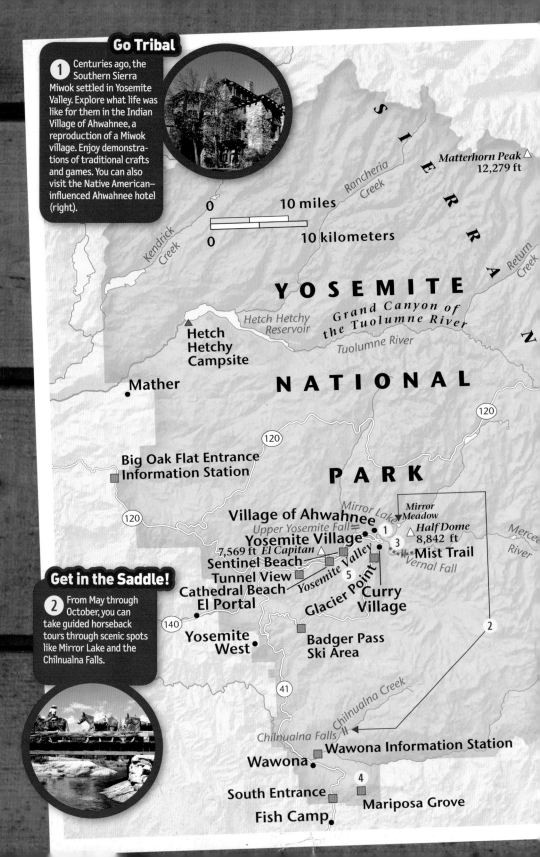

0
10 miles

0
10 kilometers

S I E R R A

△ Matterhorn Peak
12,279 ft

Kendrick Creek

Rancheria Creek

Return Creek

Y O S E M I T E

Hetch Hetchy Reservoir

Grand Canyon of the Tuolumne River

Tuolumne River

▲ Hetch Hetchy Campsite

Mather

N A T I O N A L

120

Big Oak Flat Entrance Information Station

120

P A R K

120

Mirror Lake

Village of Ahwahnee

Mirror Meadow

Upper Yosemite Fall
1

△ Half Dome
8,842 ft

Mercer River

Yosemite Village
3

7,569 ft El Capitan △
Mist Trail

Sentinel Beach
Vernal Fall

Tunnel View
Yosemite Valley
5

Cathedral Beach
Glacier Point

Curry Village

El Portal

140

Yosemite West

Badger Pass Ski Area

2

41

Chilnualna Creek

Chilnualna Falls

Wawona Information Station

Wawona

South Entrance

4

Mariposa Grove

Fish Camp

Happy Trails

3 Whether you're up for a tougher trek (like the slippery ascent to the top of Vernal Fall on the Mist Trail) or a simple stroll, some of Yosemite's 800 miles of marked hiking trails will suit your style.

Ride of a Lifetime

5 Bring your bike (or rent one when you arrive). You can cycle by some of the park's most picturesque spots on the 12 miles of mostly paved paths circling Yosemite Valley. Hang on to your handlebars!

Tioga Pass Entrance

120

YOSEMITE NATIONAL PARK

Sacramento ⊙

Sequoia National Park

Kings Canyon National Park

San Francisco ●

Death Valley National Park

CALIFORNIA

Los Angeles ●

PACIFIC OCEAN

[DARE TO EXPLORE]

PAN FOR GOLD
Pan for gold in Mariposa, about 30 miles from Yosemite and you may strike it rich while seeking the shiny stuff in a creek where gold was first found way back in 1848.
www.goldfeverprospecting.com/gopayo.html

DISCOVER YOUR INNER PHOTOGRAPHER
Learn all about one of America's most well-known photographers at the Ansel Adams Gallery, in the heart of Yosemite Valley. Pick up posters, calendars, and other items featuring Adams's iconic images—plus photography tips from the gallery's staff.
www.anseladams.com

HIT THE TRACKS
Visit the Yosemite Mountain Sugar Pine Railroad in Fish Camp, near the park's southern entrance. Take a scenic ride through the Sierra Nevada Forest on a historic steam engine, or opt for a quicker trip on the gas powered Jenny Railcar.
www.ymsprr.com

GET HANDS-ON
Explore the Children's Museum of the Sierra, located in Oakhurst, about 24 miles from Yosemite. Visit a kid-size fire station, doctor's office, bank, and pizza restaurant, and other hands-on exhibits.
www.childrensmuseumofthesierra.org

MY CHECKLIST
- ✔ Check out the rock climbers from El Capitan meadow.
- ✔ Walk to the base of Bridalveil Fall.
- ✔ Meander through Mariposa Grove.
- ✔ Snap some shots from Tunnel View.
- ✔ Gawk at Glacier Point's stunning scenery.
- ✔ Visit the Indian Village of Ahwahnee.
- ✔ Join the Junior Rangers.

Tall, Tall Trees

4 Yosemite's famous Mariposa Grove of giant sequoias (left) is home to some of the world's tallest—and oldest—trees. Two must-see trees? The Columbia, which stands taller than the Statue of Liberty, and the Wawona Tunnel Tree.

FAST FACT: Yosemite's sequoia trees are the largest living things on Earth.

Welcome to
Zion
National Park!

Zion may not be as famous

as some of its national park counter-parts, but that doesn't mean it's not as stunning. Within this lesser-explored destination in Utah, you'll find soaring cliffs, rushing waterfalls, deep green natural pools, and red sandstone canyons and rock foundations. Sitting at the junction formed by the Mojave Desert, the Colorado Plateau, and the Great Basin, Zion's unique positioning yields awe-inspiring sights, unique wildlife, and adventures everywhere you go.

State: Utah
Established: November 19, 1919
Size: 146,592 acres
Website: www.nps.gov/zion

🚗 DISCOVER ZION 🚗

RANGER TIPS

Watch your footing! Zion is filled with steep cliffs and narrow canyons (right), so stay away from the edges. In the summer temperatures can top 105°F, so be sure to carry plenty of water. ➔

TAKE IT EASY

Take a break, relax, and eat at the Grotto Picnic Area or under the shade trees near Zion Lodge. For an easy 2-mile stroll head to Riverside Walk, the park's most popular trail. This paved path will lead you past hanging gardens of green maidenhair ferns and golden columbine flowers (pictured here). ⬇

BE EXTREME

Splash and scream down the Virgin River on an inner tube. Part lazy river ride and part waterslide, you'll cool off—and get your fill of thrills—by tubing.

BEST VIEW

Hike the 1-mile Canyon Overlook Trail for a magnificent view of lower Zion Canyon (reach the trailhead at the east side of the Zion–Mount Carmel Tunnel). You can also take a drive on the Zion–Mount Carmel Highway and the Zion Canyon Scenic Drive for great views of the park (above left). Note: There is a free shuttle bus from late March to November. 🧭

ALL ABOUT ANIMALS

Zion is home to mule deer (below), lizards, ringtails, and rare species like the peregrine falcon, Mexican spotted owl, California condor, desert tortoise, and the endemic Zion snail. Visiting in the late summer or fall? Keep your eyes open for tarantulas, which emerge from their underground homes in search of mates at that time of year. ⬇

INTERSTATE 15

KOLOB
CANYONS
ROAD

△ *Horse Ranch*
Mt.
8,726 ft

■ **Kolob Canyons**
Visitor Center

Kolob
Canyons ■

K O L O B

C A N Y O N S
④

Hurricane Cleefs

La Verkin Creek

Hop Valley

Lower Kolob Plateau

Kolob
Reservoir

Upper Kolob Plateau

KOLOB
TERRACE
ROAD

■ **Lava**
Point
Overlook

Kolob Creek

Horse Pasture Plateau

North Fork Virgin Riv

RIVERSIDE WALK
Weeping Rock

Zion Canyon

③

③

LOWER EMERALD
POOL TRAIL   ③

Zion
Lodge ■

ZION CANYON SCENIC DRIVE

①

PA'RUS TRAIL

Zion Canyon Visitor Center
(Zion Canyon Field Institute) ⑤

Zion Canyon Theater ■ ②

Zion-
Mt. Car
Tunnel

■ **Canyon**
Overlook

ZION-MOUNT
CARMEL HIGHWAY

Z I O N

N A T I O N A L

P A R K

North Creek

⑨ •**Virgin**

Virgin River

Springdale •

⑨

Parunuwe
Canyon

Rockville

East Fork Virgin River

Ride of a Lifetime

② Many of Zion's roads are closed off to cars, making them perfect grounds for cycling. Rent a bike within the park and pedal around paths like the Pa'rus Trail (left), which follows the Virgin River through lower Zion Canyon.

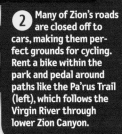

Take a Tour

① Take the Ride With the Ranger Shuttle Tour (below) on the Zion Canyon Scenic Drive. Learn tons about Zion while a knowledgeable ranger offers interesting info and fun facts along the 50-minute ride. Bonus: The shuttle buses are propane-powered, making them eco-friendly.

0 _____ 4 miles

0 _____ 4 kilometers

◎ **Salt Lake City**

U T A H

Cedar Breaks
National Monument

■ Bryce Canyon
■ National Park

□ **ZION**
NATIONAL PARK

Take a Hike

3 Zion's filled with family-friendly hikes, like the half-mile round-trip Weeping Rock Trail, where you can actually see water coming out of a rock. The shady and scenic Lower Emerald Pool Trail is another favorite. Up for something a tad tougher? Hit the East Rim, a 10-mile, one-way downhill trail that ends in Zion Canyon.

Get in the Saddle

4 Travel into Kolob Canyon on horseback, just as the pioneers did hundreds of years ago. Take a guided tour and learn from local cowboys, who offer up tales about Zion's sights and wildlife.

Learn More

EAST RIM TRAIL

9

East Entrance

5 Head to the Zion Canyon Field Institute, part of the Zion Natural History Association, where you can join an outdoor workshop on topics like photography and geology or link up with guided tours.

[DARE TO EXPLORE]

HIT THE BREAKS
Travel to Cedar Breaks National Monument, about 75 miles north of Zion National Park, to see sculpted hoodoos, spires, and colorful wildflowers in the spring. **www.nps.gov/cebr**

PARK HOP
Double your park fun by hitting Bryce Canyon National Park, about 50 miles away from Zion. Bonus: You don't even have to get in your car—the Bryce Canyon shuttle provides transportation to and from the park. **www.nps.gov/brca**

RAINY DAY?
Or maybe you just need to rest your legs after all of that hiking. In either case, stop at the Zion Canyon Giant Screen Theater for a few hours of fun. See a 3D movie on the six-story-high, 82-foot-wide screen. **www.zioncanyontheatre.com**

PIT STOP
Learn even more about the park at the Zion Canyon Visitor Center. It features a huge bookstore and cool exhibits; you can also shop for souvenirs, pick up park maps, and chat with rangers to better plan your time in Zion. **(435) 772-3256**

MY CHECKLIST

✔ Take a bike ride through the park.

✔ Cruise along the sites on the park shuttle.

✔ Ride down a canyon on horseback.

✔ Tube down the Virgin River.

✔ View the algae-green Emerald Pools.

✔ Check out the Weeping Rock.

✔ Head to the Zion Canyon Visitor Center for exhibits and info.

FAST FACT: The park's 287-foot-long Kolob Arch is one of the world's largest freestanding natural arches.

⇢ Other Must-see Park Properties in the West

ALA KAHAKAI NATIONAL HISTORIC TRAIL (HI)

www.nps.gov/alka

WHY IT'S COOL: It's a 175-mile trail through hundreds of ancient Hawaiian settlement sites.

WHAT TO DO: Hiking and exploring the temples, house site foundations, fishponds, fishing shrines, petroglyphs, sacred places, ponds, and reefs.

TRY THIS: Look for sea turtles along the shores of Anaehoomalu and Makaiwa Bays.

BIGHORN CANYON NATIONAL RECREATION AREA (MT, WY)

www.nps.gov/bica

WHY IT'S COOL: It has steep canyon walls and is home to a diversity of wildlife, including wild horses, black bears, bighorn rams, and mule deer.

WHAT TO DO: Visit historic ranches; boating, hiking, and wildlife-watching.

TRY THIS: Take your bike along South District park road, paralleling the ancient Bad Pass Trail.

CABRILLO NATIONAL MONUMENT (CA)

www.nps.gov/cabr

WHY IT'S COOL: It's the site where the first Europeans set foot on what is now the West Coast of the United States.

WHAT TO DO: Visit Old Point Loma Lighthouse; hiking, bird-watching, tide-pooling, and biking.

TRY THIS: Take a walk to the Whale Overlook to see views of the Pacific and, in the winter, views of whales.

CEDAR BREAKS NATIONAL MONUMENT (UT)

www.nps.gov/cebr

WHY IT'S COOL: It features multicolored rock formations—some 60 million years old.

WHAT TO DO: Hiking, camping, and scenic drives.

TRY THIS: Learn about the monument's amazing geology through ranger programs.

COLORADO NATIONAL MONUMENT (CO)

www.nps.gov/colm

WHY IT'S COOL: Its grand panorama of plateau and canyon offers one of the most beautiful landscapes in the West.

WHAT TO DO: Hiking, camping, bicycling, rock climbing, and wildlife-watching.

TRY THIS: Take in the scenery and red-rock canyons along the 23-mile Rim Rock Drive.

CRATERS OF THE MOON NATIONAL MONUMENT AND PRESERVE (ID)

www.nps.gov/crmo

WHY IT'S COOL: Rugged lava flows that resemble the surface of the moon.

WHAT TO DO: Climb a volcano; take a ranger-led tour; camping, hiking, backpacking, skiing, and snowshoeing.

TRY THIS: Take in exceptional views from your car by driving the 7-mile loop.

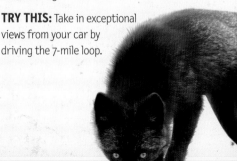

DEVILS TOWER NATIONAL MONUMENT (WY)

www.nps.gov/deto

WHY IT'S COOL: It's home to Devils Tower, an amazing geologic formation created by the intrusion of igneous material.

WHAT TO DO: Hiking trails, rock climbing, and cross-country skiing.

TRY THIS: Take the Tower Walk, which explores Devils Tower with a ranger.

DINOSAUR NATIONAL MONUMENT (CO, UT)

www.nps.gov/dino

WHY IT'S COOL: Tons of skeletons and skulls and other specimens of Jurassic-period dinosaurs have been found here.

WHAT TO DO: View rock art left by the people of the Fremont culture; hiking, camping, stargazing, and boating.

TRY THIS: Discover the park's river canyons by taking a raft trip down the Green and Yampa Rivers.

FORT VANCOUVER NATIONAL HISTORIC SITE (OR, WA)

www.nps.gov/fova

WHY IT'S COOL: This site preserves and re-creates a story of the 19th-century fur trading network.

WHAT TO DO: Tour the reconstructed trading post and attend park ranger weapons demonstrations and living history programs.

TRY THIS: Watch a cultural demonstration to learn about people, events, and practices of the past.

FOSSIL BUTTE NATIONAL MONUMENT (WY)

www.nps.gov/fobu

WHY IT'S COOL: One of the world's most abundant, detailed, and best preserved deposits of Eocene-epoch fossils.

WHAT TO DO: View fossil exhibits, take a scenic drive, join a ranger program, and assist on fossil collections.

TRY THIS: Have a picnic under the shade of aspen trees at the Chicken Creek Picnic Area.

GOLDEN GATE NATIONAL RECREATION AREA (CA)

www.nps.gov/goga

WHY IT'S COOL: Endless sights to see and things to do, like the Muir Woods National Monument, Fort Point National Historic Site, the Presidio, Nike Missile Site, and Ocean Beach.

WHAT TO DO: Visit the sights and tour historic areas and structures; hiking, swimming, camping, picnicking, and wildlife-watching.

TRY THIS: Take a boat ride to Alcatraz Island and see what life was like for prisoners who lived on "the Rock" from 1934 to 1963.

HOVENWEEP NATIONAL MONUMENT (CO, UT)

www.nps.gov/hove

WHY IT'S COOL: It protects the remains of six prehistoric Puebloan-era villages along the Utah–Colorado border.

WHAT TO DO: Tour the ancient Pueblo ruins; join a ranger-led program; hiking and camping.

TRY THIS: Stay past dark and check out the stars above Hovenweep, which still twinkle as bright today as they did 700 years ago!

KLONDIKE GOLD RUSH NATIONAL HISTORICAL PARK (AK, WA)

www.nps.gov/klgo

WHY IT'S COOL: It tells the story of the great Yukon gold rush of 1897.

WHAT TO DO: Tour historic buildings and boom-towns; hiking and camping.

TRY THIS: Ride the historic White Pass & Yukon Railroad for stunning views of the Coast Mountains.

LAKE MEAD NATIONAL RECREATION AREA (AZ, NV)

www.nps.gov/lake

WHY IT'S COOL: It's home to Lake Mead and Lake Mohave, plus acres of desert and wilderness.

WHAT TO DO: Boating, kayaking, canoeing, waterskiing, hiking, fishing, picnicking, plus exploring mountains, desert basins, and canyons.

TRY THIS: Hot day? Take a dip in the sparkling clean waters of Lake Mead and Lake Mohave.

LAKE ROOSEVELT NATIONAL RECREATION AREA (WA)

www.nps.gov/laro

WHY IT'S COOL: It provides visitors with tons of recreational opportunities along and on the beautiful river.

WHAT TO DO: Camping, boating, fishing, swimming, picnicking, and hiking.

TRY THIS: Tour the grounds of Historic Fort Spokane, a U.S. military post and an Indian boarding school.

LITTLE BIGHORN BATTLEFIELD NATIONAL MONUMENT (MT)

www.nps.gov/libi

WHY IT'S COOL: It's the site of Col. George A. Custer's "last stand" and a monument to the Sioux and Cheyenne Indians who battled there.

WHAT TO DO: Tour the battlefield and the Custer National Cemetery.

TRY THIS: Head to the visitor center and stick around for ranger-led talks on the battlefields and history.

MUIR WOODS NATIONAL MONUMENT (CA)

www.nps.gov/muwo

WHY IT'S COOL: You'll see redwood trees up to 260 feet tall, averaging 600 to 800 years of age.

WHAT TO DO: Gaze up at the giant redwoods, hike some of the park's miles of trails, learn about its diverse flora and fauna, and go on ranger-led tours.

TRY THIS: Hike the Marin Headlands, where you'll find Fort Cronkhite, a former World War II military post at the edge of the Pacific Ocean.

OREGON CAVES NATIONAL MONUMENT (OR)

www.nps.gov/orca

WHY IT'S COOL: It's home to one of the few marble caves in the world!

WHAT TO DO: Cave tours, hiking, and ranger-led programs.

TRY THIS: Hit one of the park's four hiking trails to check out views of the surrounding Siskiyou Mountains.

PUUHONUA O HONAUNAU NATIONAL HISTORICAL PARK (HI)

www.nps.gov/puho

WHY IT'S COOL: It provides a window into Hawaii's past, where the traditional life of Hawaiians is preserved and shared.

WHAT TO DO: Touring historic structures; fishing, hiking, snorkeling, wildlife-watching, and picnicking.

TRY THIS: Take a self-guided walking tour of the Royal Grounds and Puuhonua, offering a glimpse of how ancient Hawaiians lived.

SAN JUAN ISLANDS NATIONAL HISTORICAL PARK (WA)

www.nps.gov/sajh

WHY IT'S COOL: In 1859, the United States and Great Britain almost went to war when an American farmer shot a pig here, also home to more than 6 miles of shoreline.

WHAT TO DO: Hike the trails at English and American camps; study artifacts in the American Camp visitor center; kayaking, bird-watching, whale-watching, stargazing, and picking blackberries.

TRY THIS: Go tide-pooling! American Camp along the Strait of Juan de Fuca has plenty of pocket coves full of mollusks, crabs, shrimp, and more.

SANTA MONICA MOUNTAINS NATIONAL RECREATION AREA (CA)

www.nps.gov/samo

WHY IT'S COOL: Amazing mountain peaks, sandy beaches, rugged coastline, and plenty of trails, too.

WHAT TO DO: Visit historic sites; hiking, camping, and mountain biking.

TRY THIS: Check out the park on horseback by hitting some of the more than 500 miles of horse trails.

WAR IN THE PACIFIC NATIONAL HISTORICAL PARK (GU)

www.nps.gov/wapa

WHY IT'S COOL: It's a memorial to the bravery and sacrifice of the soldiers and civilians who participated in World War II's Pacific Theater.

WHAT TO DO: Visit battlefield and other historical sites; diving and snorkeling.

TRY THIS: Head up to Asan Bay Overlook for a panoramic view and its Memorial Wall, which contains 16,142 names of soldiers who suffered or died during the war on Guam.

WORLD WAR II VALOR IN THE PACIFIC NATIONAL MONUMENT (AK, CA, HI)

www.nps.gov/valr

WHY IT'S COOL: It honors those who died in the December 7, 1941, attack on the U.S. Navy base at Pearl Harbor.

WHAT TO DO: Visit the battleship memorial and battle sites, tour the museum galleries, and explore exhibits.

TRY THIS: Hop on a bike and follow the nearby Pearl Harbor bike path, which crosses through Aiea Bay park.

National Park of American Samoa

A diver swims among beautiful corals in the crystal blue water off the coast of Ofu Island in the National Park of American Samoa.

more National Parks
& Park Properties

⏩ More National Parks and Park Properties

AMERICAN SAMOA, NATIONAL PARK OF

American Samoa
Established October 31, 1988
10,520 acres
www.nps.gov/npsa

RANGER TIPS
- Want to snorkel? Bring your own equipment since beaches are remote.
- Watch for falling coconuts!
- Avoid stepping on or touching coral.

TAKE IT EASY: Spend a day relaxing at the secluded Ofu Beach.

BEST VIEW: Climb to the top of Mount Alava to get a great glimpse of the harbor and town of Pago Pago.

BE EXTREME: Explore coral reefs by snorkeling in the waters off the Ofu and Olosega beaches.

ANIMAL SIGHTINGS: Samoan flying foxes, fruit doves, and tropical fish

ARCHES NATIONAL PARK

Utah
Established November 12, 1971
76,359 acres
www.nps.gov/arch

RANGER TIPS
- Stay on trails to protect fragile desert soils and plants.
- Wear supportive shoes and watch your footing; sandstone slickrock crumbles easily.
- Don't forget your water! You'll want to drink at least a gallon a day while hiking.

TAKE IT EASY: Head to the Windows area for a series of short, easy hikes.

BEST VIEW: Stop at the Park Avenue Viewpoint for a view down an open canyon and sandstone skyscrapers.

BE EXTREME: Join the naturalist-led three-hour hike through Fiery Furnace, a dense array of rock formations that glow red as the sun sets.

ANIMAL SIGHTINGS: Mule deer, black-tailed jackrabbits, coyotes, and lizards

BISCAYNE NATIONAL PARK

Florida
Established June 28, 1980
172,924 acres
www.nps.gov/bisc

RANGER TIPS
- Don't touch coral or anything else living on the reef.
- Bring your bug spray! Mosquitoes are plentiful from April to December.
- Access to anything beyond the mainland shoreline of Biscayne requires a boat ride.

TAKE IT EASY: Enjoy a picnic along the Mangrove Shore at Convoy Point.

BEST VIEW: Check out life underneath Biscayne Bay on a reef cruise via glass-bottom boat.

BE EXTREME: Snorkel in the shallow waters and check out life on a coral reef.

ANIMAL SIGHTINGS: Shrimp, spiny lobsters, sponges, crabs, Florida manatees, and more than 325 types of fish

BLACK CANYON OF THE GUNNISON NATIONAL PARK

Colorado
Established October 21, 1999
30,385 acres
www.nps.gov/blca

RANGER TIPS

- Bring lots of water; the park's exposed trails heat up in the sun during the summer.
- If you plan to hike the inner canyon routes, you must get a permit from the visitor center first.
- Never throw anything into the canyon.

TAKE IT EASY: Follow the Rim Rock Nature Trail, a 1-mile round-trip trek offering views of the river and canyon below.

BEST VIEW: Hit High Point on the South Rim and stand 2,689 feet above the Gunnison River.

BE EXTREME: Rock climb some of the park's cliffs and canyons.

ANIMAL SIGHTINGS: Ravens, falcons, peregrine falcons, mule deer, elk, bobcats, mountain lions, and black bears

CANYONLANDS NATIONAL PARK

Utah
Established September 12, 1964
337,598 acres
www.nps.gov/cany

RANGER TIPS

- The spring and fall are ideal seasons for exploring by foot or car.
- Be extra careful around cliff edges and on slippery surfaces.
- Don't walk on the crunchy black soil seen in the park; it's composed of living plants.

TAKE IT EASY: The road to Upheaval Dome ends at a perfect picnic spot in the shade of junipers and pinyon trees.

BEST VIEW: At 6,080 feet, Grand View Point Overlook offers sweeping views of the canyons.

BE EXTREME: Bike through the park's backcountry, which is closed to cars. Check out The Needles, a collection of weathered sandstone spires.

ANIMAL SIGHTINGS: Mule deer, coyotes, porcupines, and lizards

CAPITOL REEF NATIONAL PARK

Utah
Established December 18, 1971
241,904 acres
www.nps.gov/care

RANGER TIPS

- Always check road, trail, and weather conditions before you head out on foot or by car.
- Carry in your own water, which is scarce once you enter the park.
- Pack a picnic! There's no place to buy food in the park.

TAKE IT EASY: Stop at the visitor center on the edge of Fruita to see remnants of a 120-year-old frontier community.

BEST VIEW: A 2.5-mile hike to Strike Valley Overlook in the upper Muley Twist Canyon will lead you to a vista of a canyon, double arches, and a large rock window.

BE EXTREME: Hit the Cohab Canyon Trail. This almost 2-mile hike is considered strenuous, but you'll get to climb to a hidden canyon that overlooks Fruita.

ANIMAL SIGHTINGS: Mule deer, bighorn sheep, and soaring golden eagles

CHANNEL ISLANDS NATIONAL PARK

California
Established March 5, 1980
249,354 acres
www.nps.gov/chis

RANGER TIPS

- Want to whale-watch? Hit the park from late December through March.
- Do not take anything from the boat but photos.
- Dress in layers for all types of weather.

TAKE IT EASY: Hit the beach of San Miguel, home to five seal species.

BEST VIEW: Climb the staircase to the top of the cliff on Anacapa Island and peer 150 feet below to the sea.

BE EXTREME: Take a bumpy boat ride on the Santa Barbara Channel out to Anacapa Island.

ANIMAL SIGHTINGS: Seabirds, seals, sea lions, rabbits, and lizards

CONGAREE NATIONAL PARK

South Carolina
Established 2003
24,180 acres
www.nps.gov/cong

RANGER TIPS

- Bring bug spray to ward off mosquitoes.
- Avoid all snakes—there are poisonous species in the park.
- Bring an extra set of clothes to change into after your visit—you'll probably get muddy!

TAKE IT EASY: Hit the park at night for the ranger-led "owl prowl" to hear the eerie *hoo-hoos* of owls and see the glowing fungi that grows on cypress trees.

BEST VIEW: Take the 2.4-mile Boardwalk Trail to see some of the country's tallest trees, like giant loblolly pines and old bald cypresses.

BE EXTREME: Paddle the Cedar Creek Canoe Trail and look for wildlife in the water.

ANIMAL SIGHTINGS: Bobcats, deer, river otters, woodpeckers, owls, turtles, and wild pigs

CRATER LAKE NATIONAL PARK

Oregon
Established May 22, 1902
183,244 acres
www.nps.gov/crla

RANGER TIPS

- Plan to spend at least a half-day touring the park's Rim Drive.
- Watch your footing—volcanic rock and soil are unstable and dangerous to climb on.
- Wear sturdy shoes and bring water, a snack, and a jacket.

TAKE IT EASY: Stroll down the Godfrey Glen Trail, an easy 1-mile loop leading through a forest.

BEST VIEW: Climb the Wizard Island Summit Trail to reach views of white-park pines against the lake's blue water, and a look inside a 90-foot-deep crater.

BE EXTREME: Hike 2.5 miles up the Mount Scott Trail to the park's highest point.

ANIMAL SIGHTINGS: Black bears, bobcats, deer, marmots, eagles, and hawks

DEATH VALLEY NATIONAL PARK

California/Nevada
Established October 31, 1994
About 3,400,000 acres
www.nps.gov/deva

RANGER TIPS

- Be careful of the heat. Drink lots of water, wear a hat and sunglasses, and don't venture out if the temperature is too high.
- Never enter an abandoned mineshaft or tunnel.
- Head indoors if it rains—desert storms may cause flash floods.

TAKE IT EASY: Rest and refuel at the Furnace Creek Visitor Center, featuring exhibits and a bookstore.

BEST VIEW: Drive to Zabriskie Point for awesome views of the valley.

BE EXTREME: Seasoned hikers can consider the all-day hike from Wildrose Canyon up to Telescope Peak, Death Valley's highest point at 11,049 feet.

ANIMAL SIGHTINGS: Bobcats, kit foxes, hawks, and peregrine falcons

DRY TORTUGAS NATIONAL PARK

Florida
Established October 26, 1992
64,700 acres
www.nps.gov/drto

RANGER TIPS

- Avoid travel to the park during

hurricane season (June through November).
- Want to snorkel? The visitor center has goggles, snorkels, and flippers available for loan.
- Bring your own water and food—there is nothing available within the park.

TAKE IT EASY: Stroll the grassy parapet at the Garden Key harbor light, where you can check out huge coastal guns.

BEST VIEW: Climb the spiral staircase to the top of Fort Jefferson for 360-degree views—and awesome bird-watching.

BE EXTREME: Snorkel along the 0.6-mile seawall and moat, or swim from the beach to isolated Bush Key (check with the visitor center first to make sure the key is open).

ANIMAL SIGHTINGS: Queen conch, yellow stingrays, gray snappers, sea stars, and 442 species of fish

GATES OF THE ARCTIC NATIONAL PARK AND PRESERVE

Alaska
Established December 2, 1980
8,500,000 acres
www.nps.gov/gaar

RANGER TIPS

- Layer up! The weather is unpredictable and you can expect snow or rain at any time.
- There are no visitor centers here, so bring everything you may need with you.
- Stick to the trails and avoid stepping on the fragile lichen, which takes 150 years to grow.

TAKE IT EASY: Because it's so rugged, Gates of the Arctic is recommended for highly skilled hikers only.

BEST VIEW: Climb practically any ridge of the park to see spectacular scenes of glaciers, mountains, alpine valleys, and forested lowlands.

BE EXTREME: Float down the Alatna River on a four- to seven-day wilderness trip.

ANIMAL SIGHTINGS:
Caribou, grizzly bears, wolves, wolverines, foxes, and gyrfalcons

GLACIER BAY NATIONAL PARK AND PRESERVE

Alaska
Established December 2, 1980
3,280,198 acres
www.nps.gov/glba

RANGER TIPS
- Be careful—brown bears are common, especially on Blue Mouse Cove.
- Do not get close to icebergs when boating.
- Never climb on a glacier without a guide.

TAKE IT EASY: Follow the Bartlett River Trail through a rain forest to a quiet meadow.

BEST VIEW: Go to the bay's west arm to see stunning views of the 15,300-foot Mount Fairweather.

BE EXTREME: Paddle around the bay's Muir and Adams Inlets, favorite spots of kayakers.

ANIMAL SIGHTINGS: Wolves, moose, mountain goats, bears, bald eagles, harbor seals, humpback whales, killer whales, and birds

GREAT BASIN NATIONAL PARK

Nevada
Established October 27, 1986
77,180 acres
www.nps.gov/grba

RANGER TIPS
- Beware of sudden thunderstorms that pop up any time of the year.
- Early in the morning is the best time to view Wheeler Peak.

- Stay on marked roads and trails to avoid damaging fragile alpine plants.

TAKE IT EASY: Follow a short trail to the historical Osceola Ditch, built in the late 1880s to carry water for gold mining.

BEST VIEW: Pull off at the Peak Overlook for awesome views of Wheeler Peak, dropping 1,800 feet to a glacier below.

BE EXTREME: Explore the intricate underground passages at Lehman Caves.

ANIMAL SIGHTINGS: Pack rats, cave crickets, snakes, and the rare pseudoscorpion—a spider with scorpion-like pinchers.

GREAT SAND DUNES NATIONAL PARK AND PRESERVE

Colorado
Established September 13, 2004
107,000 acres
www.nps.gov/grsa

RANGER TIPS
- When climbing the dunes, take your time and angle up the ridgelines of the dunes instead of climbing straight up.
- Wear shoes! The sand can reach blistering temperatures.
- Protect yourself from the sun with a hat, sunglasses, sunscreen, and plenty of water.

TAKE IT EASY: Splash along the Medano Creek, which meanders along the base of the dunes.

BEST VIEW: Make the trek up to High Dune, towering 650 feet above the San Luis Valley and offering a panorama of mountains, dunes, and valley.

BE EXTREME: Run and slide down the steep faces of the giant dunes, some reaching up to 750 feet tall.

ANIMAL SIGHTINGS: Mule deer, bighorn

sheep, chipmunks, desert cottontails, coyotes, magpies, and chickadees

GUADALUPE MOUNTAINS NATIONAL PARK

Texas
Established September 30, 1972
86,416 acres
www.nps.gov/gumo

RANGER TIPS

- Pick up maps and trail information at the Headquarters Visitor Center.
- Canyon plants are fragile; be sure to stay on the trails.
- Keep your eye open for harmful desert animals like rattlesnakes.

TAKE IT EASY: Walk the easy 2.3-mile loop trail to Smith and Manzanita Springs to familiarize yourself with the plants of the Chihuahan Desert.

BEST VIEWS: Take the Bush Mountain Trail, leading to spectacular views of the Guadalupes and the Cornudas Mountains.

BE EXTREME: Hike Devils Hall, a 4.3-mile round-trip trek down a steep, narrow canyon.

ANIMAL SIGHTINGS: Snakes, golden eagles, tarantulas (in the fall), and hummingbirds

ISLE ROYALE NATIONAL PARK

Michigan
Established April 3, 1940
571, 790 acres
www.nps.gov/isro

RANGER TIPS

- Pack in what you need and carry out your waste and trash.
- Any water collected in the park must be boiled or filtered before you drink it.
- The best way to see the park is by

backpacking to campsites; noncampers can explore on tour boats or on foot.

TAKE IT EASY: Visiting in July or August? Pick blueberries and thimbleberries in the park's lush green meadows.

BEST VIEWS: Climb to Scoville Point to view some of the rocky islets that form the beautiful Isle Royale archipelago.

BE EXTREME: Take a three- to five-day backpacking trip into the backcountry to see exclusive sights of the park.

ANIMAL SIGHTINGS: Wolves, moose, and foxes

KATMAI NATIONAL PARK AND PRESERVE

Alaska
Established December 2, 1980
4,725,188 acres
www.nps.gov/katm

RANGER TIPS

- Stick to the bear-viewing platforms—never go near a bear.
- Be extra careful when crossing glacial streams.
- Always kayak with a guide.

TAKE IT EASY: Take the bus or van tour to the Valley of Ten Thousand Smokes to see stunning scenery.

BEST VIEW: Watch bears feeding on jumping fish from the platform at Brooks Falls.

BE EXTREME: Kayak or canoe in the Bay of Islands in the North Arm of Naknek Lake.

ANIMAL SIGHTINGS: Alaskan brown bears, gray wolves, moose, caribou, porcupines, beavers, sea lions, sea otters, and hair seals. You may also spot beluga, killer, and gray whales along the coast.

KENAI FJORDS NATIONAL PARK

Alaska
Established December 2, 1980
607,000 acres
www.nps.gov/kefj

RANGER TIPS
- Kenai's icefields are very cold year-round. Dress appropriately.
- Respect the glaciers by keeping your distance. Remember, they're moving bodies of ice and parts may break off.
- Beware of brown bears and moose.

TAKE IT EASY: Take a boat tour down Resurrection Bay and look for sea lions as you pass the Chriswell Islands.

BEST VIEW: Follow the Main Trail from the Seward Information Center for glacier and ice-field views.

BE EXTREME: Kayak the Granite Passage, an exciting entrance into Harris Bay.

ANIMAL SIGHTINGS: Harbor seals, sea lions, sea otters, moose, black bears, mountain goats, wolverines, lynx, bald eagles, puffins, peregrine falcons, and about 20 species of seabirds

KINGS CANYON NATIONAL PARK

California
Established March 4, 1940
865,257 acres
www.nps.gov/seki

RANGER TIPS

- Watch your footing around rivers and streams. The rocks can be very slippery.
- Look out for falling pinecones!
- You may gather a few pinecones or rocks from the Sequoia National Forest area only. Taking items from Kings Canyon is not allowed.

TAKE IT EASY: Walk or bike to Cedar Grove Village, a beautiful hidden valley.

BEST VIEW: Drive up to Panoramic Point to see stretches of the Sierra Nevada and the Great Western Divide.

BE EXTREME: Explore the marble Crystal Cave via a twisting, one-hour underground tour.

ANIMAL SIGHTINGS: Marmots, pikas, gray foxes, bobcats, striped and spotted skunks, black bears, birds, snakes, and lizards

KOBUK VALLEY NATIONAL PARK

Alaska
Established December 2, 1980
1,750,000 acres
www.nps.gov/kova

RANGER TIPS
- Bring everything you need

with you—there are no facilities.
- Take a guide along unless you are very experienced in the wilderness.
- Respect the activities of the Inuit people, who own much of the land along the river.

TAKE IT EASY: Take an easy canoe ride down the wide and gentle Kobuk River.

BEST VIEW: Climb to the top of the Great Kobuk Sand Dunes for a look at the amazing landscape.

BE EXTREME: Take a river-hiking trip.

ANIMAL SIGHTINGS: Brown bears, black bears, wolves, coyotes, and foxes

LAKE CLARK NATIONAL PARK AND PRESERVE

Alaska
Established December 2, 1980
4,045,000 acres
www.nps.gov/lacl

RANGER TIPS
- Hit Lake Clark in the summer to see its beautiful (and famous) wildflowers.
- Plan ahead—you can only reach this park by boat or air taxi.
- Experienced hikers only: You have to have good wilderness skills to hike, camp, or fish here.

TAKE IT EASY: Lake Clark fishing is top-notch. Cast your line into the lakes or river and relax while waiting for fish (like trout and five kinds of salmon) to bite.

BEST VIEW: Climb the 2.5-mile Tanalian Falls Trail through a forest, past bogs, and up a river to see these stunning falls.

BE EXTREME: Take a two-day rafting trip down the wild and scenic Tanalian or Tazimina Rivers.

ANIMAL SIGHTINGS: Moose, arctic ground squirrels, caribou, coyotes, wolves, lynx, river otters, wolverines, and 125 species of birds. Look

for sea lions, beluga whales, harbor seals, and porpoises in the nearby bays.

LASSEN VOLCANIC NATIONAL PARK

California
Established August 9, 1916
106,372 acres
www.nps.gov/lavo

RANGER TIPS
- View the volcanoes in the summer and fall.
- Carry water, wear a hat, and take a jacket.
- Before you set out on a hike, take some time to acclimate to the park's high elevations.

TAKE IT EASY: Visit the Loomis Museum at Manzanita Lake to learn more about the area.

BEST VIEW: Drive the park's main road for up-close looks at the park's volcanic features.

BE EXTREME: Hike the Lassen Peak Trail, a tough 5-mile round-trip climb that brings you to 8,463 feet at the summit of the active volcano.

ANIMAL SIGHTINGS: Ground squirrels, tortoiseshell butterflies, frogs, newts, and 195 species of birds

MAMMOTH CAVE NATIONAL PARK

Kentucky
Established July 1, 1941
52,830 acres
www.nps.gov/maca

RANGER TIPS
- Wear shoes with nonskid soles and long pants while exploring the cave.
- Temperatures in the cave are cool, so bring an extra layer of clothing.
- Cave tours are tough. Make sure you're up to the task before starting your journey.

TAKE IT EASY: Stop for lunch at the Snowball Room in the Cleveland Avenue section, featuring

snowball-like formations on the roof.

BEST VIEW: Stare into the 105-foot-deep Bottomless Pit.

BE EXTREME: Sign up for the Wild Cave Tour, a 5-mile, six-hour, belly-crawling journey into the cave.

ANIMAL SIGHTINGS: Deer, bobcats, foxes, muskrats, flying squirrels, raccoons, skunks, mink, lizards, turtles, snakes, salamanders, toads, frogs, lizards, and many birds

MESA VERDE NATIONAL PARK

Colorado
Established June 29, 1906
52,074 acres
www.nps.gov/meve

RANGER TIPS
- Bring binoculars! They'll come in handy when you want to peer across the canyons.
- Visiting the cliff dwellings? Wear sturdy shoes and be prepared for some tough climbs.
- Never get too close to the edge of cliff trails and canyon rims.

TAKE IT EASY: Visit the Chapin Mesa Museum for guides to the major sites and exhibits about the Mesa Verde people.

BEST VIEW: Drive to Sun Point Overlook to see a bunch of cliff dwellings, like Cliff Palace, Sunset House, and Mummy House.

BE EXTREME: Scale a 32-foot ladder to reach Balcony House, a 40-room dwelling that requires a crawl through a tunnel to exit.

ANIMAL SIGHTINGS: Coyotes, gray foxes, mountain lions, black bears, elk, marmots, porcupines, jackrabbits, and owls

NORTH CASCADES NATIONAL PARK

Washington
Established October 2, 1968
684,000 acres
www.nps.gov/noca

RANGER TIPS
- Summer gives you the best access to the park and its activities.
- Bring binoculars to spot climbers and mountain goats on the granite faces of the Cascade peaks.
- Boat tours require a reservation; make yours at least a month in advance.

TAKE IT EASY: Take City Light's 2.5-hour boat tour of Diablo Lake.

BEST VIEW: Stop at the Washington Pass Overlook for an amazing view of Cascade peaks, including the 7,740-foot Early Winter Spires.

BE EXTREME: Take the rugged and steep Horseshoe Basin Trail, a 3.9-mile trek passing more than 15 waterfalls as glaciers and mountains loom in the background.

ANIMAL SIGHTINGS: Columbia black-tailed deer, Douglas squirrels, pikas, mountain goats, reptiles, amphibians, and bald eagles

PETRIFIED FOREST NATIONAL PARK

Arizona
Established December 9, 1962
93,533 acres
www.nps.gov/pefo

RANGER TIPS
- Visit in the fall to enjoy the mild weather.

- Get out of your car! Plan enough time to walk among the fossil logs and Painted Desert badlands.
- Resist the urge to take a piece of petrified wood with you and leave with only memories from the park.

TAKE IT EASY: Walk the 0.6-mile Long Logs loop to see the largest concentration of petrified wood in the park.

BEST VIEW: Pull off at Pintado Point to see panoramic views of the Lithodendron Wash, the Black Forest, and Pilot Rock—the park's highest point.

BE EXTREME: Seek out the elusive Onyx Bridge in the Petrified Forest National Wilderness Area. With no trails and no landmarks to guide you, locating the bridge is an adventure!

ANIMAL SIGHTINGS: Lizards, snakes, toads, salamanders, coyotes, foxes, bobcats, mule deer, pronghorn, ringtails, raccoons, badgers, skunks, jackrabbits, and birds

REDWOOD **NATIONAL PARK**

California
Established October 2, 1968
131,983 acres, including 3 state parks
www.nps.gov/redw

RANGER TIPS
- Think about a trip in the spring or fall to avoid crowds.
- Play it safe and stay out of the ocean—the cold water and strong undertow make swimming dangerous.
- Protect the park's wildlife by avoiding feeding all animals.

TAKE IT EASY: Picnic and relax at Hidden Beach, off the Coastal Trail along the shores of the Pacific Ocean.

BEST VIEWS: Check out Crescent Beach Overlook for outstanding ocean views and to

spot migrating gray whales in the fall or spring.

BE EXTREME: Brave the rapids of Klamath River on a kayak.

ANIMAL SIGHTINGS: Elk, pelicans, gulls, bobcats, black bears, gray foxes, and northern spotted owls

SAGUARO **NATIONAL PARK**

Arizona
Established October 14, 1994
91,445 acres
www.nps.gov/sagu

RANGER TIPS
- Always stay on the trails.
- If out at night, carry a flashlight to avoid encounters with unsuspecting wildlife.
- Pack plenty of water and snacks for hikes.

TAKE IT EASY: Grab lunch and check out centuries-old petroglyphs etched in the rocks in the Signal Hill Picnic Area.

BEST VIEWS: Head to the top of Valley View Overlook Trail to get a great view of the cactus-covered land below.

BE EXTREME: Hop on a mountain bike and pedal your way down Cactus Forest Trail, a 2.5-mile dirt trail rolling by desert scrub and sagebrush.

ANIMAL SIGHTINGS: Desert tortoises, desert iguanas, horned lizards, Gila monsters, six species of rattlesnakes, and black bears

SEQUOIA NATIONAL PARK

California
Established September 25, 1890
865,257 acres
www.nps.gov/seki

RANGER TIPS

- Hit the trails and take a hike for the park's best vantage points.
- Pack a magnifying glass in your backpack so you can see some of the smaller things living in Sequoia.
- Wear layers and bring a jacket with you—the weather and temperatures can vary throughout the park.
- Avoid run-ins with wildlife by keeping your food properly stored and picking up all of your trash.

TAKE IT EASY: Stroll the Congress Trail, which will lead you past some of the park's most famous trees.

BEST VIEWS: Climb to the top of Moro Rock, high above the tall sequoia trees. On a clear day, you can see 100 miles west.

BE EXTREME: Explore Crystal Cave, requiring

a 15-minute hike down a steep path to the cave entrance.

ANIMAL SIGHTINGS: Bobcats, foxes, coyotes, squirrels, mule deer, frogs, beavers, turtles, and snakes. Black bears and mountain lions also call Sequoia home.

SHENANDOAH NATIONAL PARK

Virginia
Established December 26, 1935
197,411 acres
www.nps.gov/shen

RANGER TIPS
- Watch your footing on the slippery rocks around waterfalls.
- Avoid chasing and feeding the wildlife.
- Arrive early to avoid traffic jams on Skyline Drive.

TAKE IT EASY: Take a breather at the Dickey Ridge Picnic Area off Skyline Drive, a scenic spot within walking distance to hiking trails.

BEST VIEWS: Stop at Crescent Rock Overlook for a look at Hawksbill Mountain, the highest peak in the park. A challenging climb to the top of Bearfence Mountain rewards you with an awesome 360-degree view.

BE EXTREME: With an adult's supervision, take a dip in one of the park's many swimming holes, like the Hughes River in Nicholson Hollow.

ANIMAL SIGHTINGS: Opossums, gray foxes, bobcats, raccoons, black bears, white-tailed deer, salamanders, turtles, snakes, barred owls, red-tailed hawks, warblers, and woodpeckers

VIRGIN ISLANDS NATIONAL PARK

United States Virgin Islands
Established August 2, 1956
15,135 acres
www.nps.gov/viis

RANGER TIPS

- Wear water shoes while wading to avoid stepping on sharp shells and coral.
- Bring plenty of bug spray, sunscreen, water, and snacks.
- Visiting in the winter? Hit the Francis Bay Trail for spectacular bird-watching.

TAKE IT EASY: Wiggle your toes in the sands of the park's famous beaches, like Hawksnest Bay, Trunk Bay, and Cinnamon Bay.

BEST VIEWS: Hike to the end of the Ram Head Trail for a sweeping view of the Caribbean Sea from a height of 200 feet.

BE EXTREME: Snorkel along an underwater nature trail in Trunk Bay.

ANIMAL SIGHTINGS: Sea turtles, pelicans, frigatebirds, mongooses, and a rainbow of tropical fish

VOYAGEURS NATIONAL PARK

Minnesota
Established April 8, 1975
218,054 acres
www.nps.gov/voya

RANGER TIPS

- Always wear a life jacket when you're on the water. It's the law!
- Avoid attracting bears by keeping your food properly stored and carrying all of your garbage out of the park with you.
- Don't drink the lake water unless you filter it first.

TAKE IT EASY: Park your car by the Ash River Visitor Center, where you can relax in the shade before hiking to the Voyageurs Forest Overlook.

BEST VIEWS: Take a 2-mile hike to the Anderson Bay Overlook, offering a cliff-top view of sparkling Rainy Lake.

BE EXTREME: In the summer, launch a kayak down any of the park's 45 miles of water-accessible trails. In the winter, catch a ride on a snowmobile or explore the area on cross-country skis.

ANIMAL SIGHTINGS: Bald eagles, wolves, muskrats, loons, blue-winged teal, and beavers

WRANGELL–ST. ELIAS NATIONAL PARK AND PRESERVE

Alaska
Established December 2, 1980
13,188,000 acres
www.nps.gov/wrst

RANGER TIPS

- When to head to Wrangell–St. Elias? Think summer. June is best for wildflowers; July has the warmest days; berries ripen in August.
- Bring bug spray, a head net, and an insect-proof tent to protect against mosquitoes in the summer.
- On clear, cold days look for steam plumes rising from Mount Wrangell, an active volcano.

TAKE IT EASY: Stop at the McCarthy Lodge for a mouthwatering meal of fresh fish and locally grown produce or pack a picnic and spread it out at the Liberty Falls campground area.

BEST VIEWS: The windy, rocky McCarthy Road dead-ends at an eye-popping overlook of four rivers, lakes, forest, snowcapped mountains, and more.

BE EXTREME: Shoot the rapids of Copper River on a guided raft trip.

ANIMAL SIGHTINGS: Grizzly and black bears, moose, elk, bald eagles, game fish, sheep, caribou, goats, coyotes, red foxes, wolverines, and porcupines

⟫ National Park Properties by State

ALABAMA

- Horseshoe Bend National Military Park
- Little River Canyon National Preserve
- Russell Cave National Monument
- Tuskegee Airmen National Historic Site
- Tuskegee Institute National Historic Site

ALASKA

- Alagnak Wild River
- Aniakchak National Monument and Preserve
- Cape Krusenstern National Monument
- Klondike Gold Rush National Historical Park
  (a separate part of the park is in WA)
- Noatak National Preserve
- Sitka National Historical Park
- Yukon–Charley Rivers National Preserve

ARIZONA

- Canyon de Chelly National Monument
- Casa Grande Ruins National Monument
- Chiricahua National Monument
- Coronado National Memorial
- Fort Bowie National Historic Site
- Glen Canyon National Recreation Area (spans into UT)
- Grand Canyon–Parashant National Monument
- Hohokam Pima National Monument
- Hubbell Trading Post National Historic Site
- Lake Mead National Recreation Area (spans into NV)
- Montezuma Castle National Monument
- Navajo National Monument
- Organ Pipe Cactus National Monument
- Pipe Spring National Monument
- Sunset Crater Volcano National Monument
- Tonto National Monument
- Tumacácori National Historical Park
- Tuzigoot National Monument
- Walnut Canyon National Monument
- Wupatki National Monument

ARKANSAS

- Arkansas Post National Memorial
- Buffalo National River

- Fort Smith National Historic Site (spans into OK)
- Little Rock Central High School National Historic Site
- Pea Ridge National Military Park
- President William Jefferson Clinton Birthplace Home National Historic Site

CALIFORNIA

- Cabrillo National Monument
- Devils Postpile National Monument
- Eugene O'Neill National Historic Site
- Fort Point National Historic Site
- Golden Gate National Recreation Area
- John Muir National Historic Site
- Lava Beds National Monument
- Manzanar National Historic Site
- Mojave National Preserve
- Muir Woods National Monument
- Pinnacles National Monument
- Point Reyes National Seashore
- Port Chicago Naval Magazine National Memorial
- Rosie the Riveter/World War II Home Front National Historical Park
- San Francisco Maritime National Historical Park
- Santa Monica Mountains National Recreation Area
- Whiskeytown National Recreation Area

COLORADO

- Bent's Old Fort National Historic Site
- Colorado National Monument
- Curecanti National Recreation Area
- Dinosaur National Monument (spans into UT)
- Florissant Fossil Beds National Monument
- Hovenweep National Monument (spans into UT)
- Sand Creek Massacre National Historic Site
- Yucca House National Monument

CONNECTICUT

- Weir Farm National Historic Site

DELAWARE

- None

DISTRICT OF COLUMBIA

- Battleground National Cemetery
- Carter G. Woodson Home National Historic Site

- Chesapeake & Ohio Canal National Historical Park (spans into MD, WV)
- Constitution Gardens
- Ford's Theatre National Historic Site
- Franklin Delano Roosevelt Memorial
- Frederick Douglass National Historic Site
- Korean War Veterans Memorial
- Lincoln Memorial
- Lyndon Baines Johnson Memorial Grove-on-the-Potomac
- Martin Luther King, Jr., Memorial
- Mary McLeod Bethune Council House National Historic Site
- National Capital Parks-East (spans into MD)
- National Mall and Memorial Parks
- Pennsylvania Avenue National Historic Site
- Rock Creek Park
- Theodore Roosevelt Island National Memorial
- Thomas Jefferson Memorial
- Vietnam Veterans Memorial
- Washington Monument
- White House
- World War II Memorial

FLORIDA

- Big Cypress National Preserve
- Canaveral National Seashore
- Castillo de San Marcos National Monument
- De Soto National Memorial
- Fort Caroline National Memorial
- Fort Matanzas National Monument
- Gulf Islands National Seashore (spans into MS)
- Timucuan Ecological and Historic Preserve

GEORGIA

- Andersonville National Cemetery
- Andersonville National Historic Site
- Chattahoochee River National Recreation Area
- Chickamauga and Chattanooga National Military Park (spans into TN)
- Cumberland Island National Seashore
- Fort Frederica National Monument
- Fort Pulaski National Monument
- Jimmy Carter National Historic Site
- Kennesaw Mountain National Battlefield Park

- Martin Luther King, Jr., National Historic Site
- Ocmulgee National Monument

GUAM

- War in the Pacific National Historical Park

HAWAII

- Kalaupapa National Historical Park
- Kaloko-Honokohau National Historical Park
- Pu'uhonua o Honaunau National Historical Park
- Pu'ukohola Heiau National Historic Site
- WWII Valor in the Pacific National Monument (spans into AK, CA)

IDAHO

- City of Rocks National Reserve
- Craters of the Moon National Monument and Preserve
- Hagerman Fossil Beds National Monument
- Minidoka National Historic Site
- Nez Perce National Historical Park (spans into MT, OR, WA)

ILLINOIS

- Lincoln Home National Historic Site

INDIANA

- George Rogers Clark National Historical Park
- Indiana Dunes National Lakeshore
- Lincoln Boyhood National Memorial

IOWA

- Effigy Mounds National Monument
- Herbert Hoover National Historic Site

KANSAS

- Brown v. Board of Education National Historic Site
- Fort Larned National Historic Site
- Fort Scott National Historic Site
- Nicodemus National Historic Site
- Tallgrass Prairie National Preserve

KENTUCKY

- Abraham Lincoln Birthplace National Historical Park
- Big South Fork National River and Recreation Area

(spans into TN)
- Cumberland Gap National Historical Park (spans into TN, VA)
- Fort Donelson National Battlefield (spans into TN)

LOUISIANA

- Cane River Creole National Historical Park
- Chalmette National Cemetery
- Jean Lafitte National Historical Park and Preserve
- New Orleans Jazz National Historical Park
- Poverty Point National Monument

MAINE

- None

MARYLAND

- Antietam National Battlefield
- Antietam National Cemetery
- Assateague Island National Seashore (spans into VA)
- Catoctin Mountain Park
- Chesapeake & Ohio Canal National Historical Park (spans into DC, WV)
- Clara Barton National Historic Site
- Fort McHenry National Monument and Historic Shrine
- Hampton National Historic Site
- Monocacy National Battlefield
- National Capital Park-East (spans into DC)
- Thomas Stone National Historic Site

MASSACHUSETTS

- Adams National Historical Park
- Boston African American National Historic Site
- Boston Harbor Islands National Recreation Area
- Boston National Historical Park
- Cape Cod National Seashore
- Frederick Law Olmsted National Historic Site
- John Fitzgerald Kennedy National Historic Site
- Longfellow House–Washington's Headquarters National Historic Site
- Lowell National Historical Park
- Minute Man National Historical Park
- New Bedford Whaling National Historical Park
- Salem Maritime National Historic Site
- Saugus Iron Works National Historic Site
- Springfield Armory National Historic Site

MICHIGAN

- Keweenaw National Historical Park
- Pictured Rocks National Lakeshore
- River Raisin National Battlefield Park
- Sleeping Bear Dunes National Lakeshore

MINNESOTA

- Grand Portage National Monument
- Mississippi National River and Recreation Area
- Pipestone National Monument
- Saint Croix National Scenic Riverway (spans into WI)

MISSISSIPPI

- Brices Cross Roads National Battlefield
- Gulf Islands National Seashore (spans into FL)
- Natchez National Historical Park
- Natchez Trace Parkway
- Tupelo National Battlefield
- Vicksburg National Cemetery
- Vicksburg National Military Park (spans into LA)

MISSOURI

- George Washington Carver National Monument
- Harry S Truman National Historic Site
- Jefferson National Expansion Memorial
- Ozark National Scenic Riverways
- Ulysses S. Grant National Historic Site
- Wilson's Creek National Battlefield

MONTANA

- Big Hole National Battlefield
- Bighorn Canyon National Recreation Area (spans into WY)
- Custer National Cemetery
- Fort Union Trading Post National Historic Site (spans into ND)
- Grant-Kohrs Ranch National Historic Site
- Little Bighorn Battlefield National Monument
- Nez Perce National Historical Park (spans into ID, OR, WA)

NEBRASKA

- Agate Fossil Beds National Monument
- Homestead National Monument of America
- Missouri National Recreational River (spans into SD)

- Niobrara National Scenic River
- Scotts Bluff National Monument

NEVADA
- Lake Mead National Recreation Area (spans into AZ)

NEW HAMPSHIRE
- Saint-Gaudens National Historic Site

NEW JERSEY
- Delaware Water Gap National Recreation Area (spans into PA)
- Gateway National Recreation Area (spans into NY)
- Great Egg Harbor Scenic and Recreational River
- Morristown National Historical Park
- Statue of Liberty National Monument (spans into NY)
- Thomas Edison National Historical Park

NEW MEXICO
- Aztec Ruins National Monument
- Bandelier National Monument
- Capulin Volcano National Monument
- Chaco Culture National Historical Park
- El Malpais National Monument
- El Morro National Monument
- Fort Union National Monument
- Gila Cliff Dwellings National Monument
- Pecos National Historical Park
- Petroglyph National Monument
- Salinas Pueblo Missions National Monument
- White Sands National Monument

NEW YORK
- African Burial Ground National Monument
- Castle Clinton National Monument
- Eleanor Roosevelt National Historic Site
- Federal Hall National Memorial
- Fire Island National Seashore
- Fort Stanwix National Monument
- Gateway National Recreation Area (spans into NJ)
- General Grant National Memorial
- Governors Island National Monument
- Hamilton Grange National Memorial
- Home of Franklin D. Roosevelt National Historic Site
- Martin Van Buren National Historic Site
- Sagamore Hill National Historic Site

- Saint Paul's Church National Historic Site
- Saratoga National Historical Park
- Statue of Liberty National Monument (spans into NJ)
- Theodore Roosevelt Birthplace National Historic Site
- Theodore Roosevelt Inaugural National Historic Site
- Upper Delaware Scenic and Recreational River (spans into PA)
- Vanderbilt Mansion National Historic Site
- Women's Rights National Historical Park

NORTH CAROLINA
- Blue Ridge Parkway
- Cape Hatteras National Seashore
- Cape Lookout National Seashore
- Carl Sandburg Home National Historic Site
- Fort Raleigh National Historic Site
- Guilford Courthouse National Military Park
- Moores Creek National Battlefield
- Wright Brothers National Memorial

NORTH DAKOTA
- Fort Union Trading Post National Historic Site (spans into MT)
- Knife River Indian Villages National Historic Site

OHIO
- Dayton Aviation Heritage National Historical Park
- First Ladies National Historic Site
- Hopewell Culture National Historical Park
- James A. Garfield National Historic Site
- Perry's Victory and International Peace Memorial
- William Howard Taft National Historic Site

OKLAHOMA
- Chickasaw National Recreation Area
- Fort Smith National Historic Site (spans into AR)
- Washita Battlefield National Historic Site

OREGON
- Fort Vancouver National Historic Site (spans into WA)
- John Day Fossil Beds National Monument
- Lewis and Clark National and State Historical Parks (spans into WA)
- Nez Perce National Historical Park (spans into ID, MT, WA)
- Oregon Caves National Monument

PENNSYLVANIA

- Allegheny Portage Railroad National Historic Site
- Delaware Water Gap National Recreation Area (spans into NJ)
- Edgar Allan Poe National Historic Site
- Eisenhower National Historic Site
- Flight 93 National Memorial
- Fort Necessity National Battlefield
- Friendship Hill National Historic Site
- Gettysburg National Cemetery
- Gettysburg National Military Park
- Hopewell Furnace National Historic Site
- Independence National Historical Park
- Johnstown Flood National Memorial
- Middle Delaware National Scenic River (spans into NJ)
- Steamtown National Historic Site
- Thaddeus Kosciuszko National Memorial
- Upper Delaware Scenic and Recreational River (spans into NY)
- Valley Forge National Historical Park

PUERTO RICO

- San Juan National Historic Site

RHODE ISLAND

- Roger Williams National Memorial

SOUTH CAROLINA

- Charles Pinckney National Historic Site
- Cowpens National Battlefield
- Fort Sumter National Monument
- Kings Mountain National Military Park
- Ninety Six National Historic Site

SOUTH DAKOTA

- Jewel Cave National Monument
- Minuteman Missile National Historic Site
- Missouri National Recreational River (spans into NE)
- Mount Rushmore National Memorial

TENNESSEE

- Andrew Johnson National Cemetery
- Andrew Johnson National Historic Site
- Big South Fork National River and Recreation Area (spans into KY)
- Chickamauga and Chattanooga National Military Park (spans into GA)
- Cumberland Gap National Historical Park (spans into KY, VA)
- Fort Donelson National Battlefield (spans into KY)
- Fort Donelson National Cemetery
- Obed Wild and Scenic River
- Shiloh National Cemetery
- Shiloh National Military Park
- Stones River National Battlefield
- Stones River National Cemetery

TEXAS

- Alibates Flint Quarries National Monument
- Amistad National Recreation Area
- Big Thicket National Preserve
- Chamizal National Memorial
- Fort Davis National Historic Site
- Lake Meredith National Recreation Area
- Lyndon B. Johnson National Historical Park
- Padre Island National Seashore
- Palo Alto Battlefield National Historical Park
- Rio Grande Wild and Scenic River
- San Antonio Missions National Historical Park

U.S. VIRGIN ISLANDS

- Buck Island Reef National Monument
- Christiansted National Historic Site
- Salt River Bay National Historical Park and Ecological Preserve
- Virgin Islands Coral Reef National Monument

UTAH

- Cedar Breaks National Monument
- Dinosaur National Monument (spans into CO)
- Glen Canyon National Recreation Area (spans into AZ)
- Golden Spike National Historic Site
- Hovenweep National Monument (spans into CO)
- Natural Bridges National Monument
- Rainbow Bridge National Monument
- Timpanogos Cave National Monument

VERMONT

- Marsh-Billings-Rockefeller National Historical Park

VIRGINIA

- Appomattox Court House National Historical Park
- Arlington House, The Robert E. Lee Memorial
- Arlington National Cemetery
- Assateague Island National Seashore (spans into MD)
- Booker T. Washington National Monument
- Cedar Creek and Belle Grove National Historical Park
- Colonial National Historical Park
- Cumberland Gap National Historical Park (spans into KY, TN)
- Fredericksburg National Cemetery
- Fredericksburg and Spotsylvania County Battlefields Memorial National Military Park
- George Washington Birthplace National Monument
- Maggie L. Walker National Historic Site
- Malvern Hill, Richmond National Battlefield Park
- Manassas National Battlefield Park
- Petersburg National Battlefield
- Poplar Grove National Cemetery
- Prince William Forest Park
- Richmond National Battlefield Park
- Wolf Trap National Park for the Performing Arts
- Yorktown National Cemetery

WASHINGTON

- Ebey's Landing National Historical Reserve
- Fort Vancouver National Historic Site (spans into OR)
- Klondike Gold Rush National Historical Park (spans into AK)
- Lake Chelan National Recreation Area
- Lake Roosevelt National Recreation Area
- Lewis and Clark National and State Historical Parks (spans into OR)
- Nez Perce National Historical Park (spans into ID, MT, OR)
- Ross Lake National Recreation Area
- San Juan Islands National Historical Park
- Whitman Mission National Historic Site

WEST VIRGINIA

- Bluestone National Scenic River
- Chesapeake & Ohio Canal National Historical Park (spans into DC, MD)
- Gauley River National Recreation Area
- Harpers Ferry National Historical Park

- New River Gorge National River

WISCONSIN

- Apostle Islands National Lakeshore
- Saint Croix National Scenic Riverway (spans into MN)

WYOMING

- Bighorn Canyon National Recreation Area (spans into MT)
- Devils Tower National Monument
- Fort Butte National Monument
- Fort Laramie National Historic Site
- Fossil Butte National Monument

NATIONAL TRAILS

- Ala Kahakai National Historic Trail (HI)
- Appalachian Trail (ME to GA)
- California National Historic Trail (MO to CA)
- Captain John Smith Chesapeake National Historic Trail (DE to DC to MD to VA)
- El Camino Real de los Tejas National Historic Trail (LA to TX)
- El Camino Real de Tierra Adentro National Historic Trail (NM)
- Ice Age National Scenic Trail (WI)
- Juan Bautista de Anza National Historic Trail (AZ to CA)
- Lewis and Clark National Historic Trail (MO to OR)
- Mormon Pioneer National Historic Trail (MO to UT)
- Natchez Trace Trail (MS to TN)
- New Jersey Coastal Heritage Trail (NJ)
- North Country National Scenic Trail (NY to ND)
- Old Spanish National Historic Trail (NM to CA)
- Oregon National Historic Trail (MO to OR)
- Overmountain Victory National Historic Trail (VA to TN to NC to SC)
- Pony Express National Historic Trail (MO to CA)
- Potomac Heritage National Scenic Trail (VA to MD to PA to DC)
- Santa Fe National Historic Trail (MO to NM)
- Selma to Montgomery National Historic Trail (AL)
- Star-Spangled Banner National Historic Trail (DC to MD to VA)
- Trail of Tears National Historic Trail (TN to OK)

Glossary

archaeology: The science that deals with past human life and culture through the recovery of material remains, such as artifacts

artifact: An object or tool created by humans

biodiversity: The number of different species of plants and animals that live in a specific environment

canyon: A deep, narrow valley with steep sides

cave: A natural underground chamber that opens to the Earth's surface

cliff: A very steep rock face, usually along a coast but also on the side of a mountain

climate: Average weather conditions of a region

crater: A bowl-shaped hole in the Earth's surface caused by an explosion or the impact of another object

culture: The entire way of life shared by a group of people, including customs and beliefs

ecology: The science that deals with the relationship between living things and their environment

ecosystem: A system of living things that live together and interact with their environment

endangered: Plants or animals that are in danger of no longer being found in the wild because of loss of habitat or danger from humans

extinct: Plants or animals that have died out and no longer live on Earth

fossil: Preserved remains or traces of ancient plants and animals

geology: The study of the physical history of the Earth, its composition, its structure, and the processes that form and change it

geyser: A hot spring through which jets of water and steam erupt

glacier: A large, slow-moving mass of ice that forms over time from snow

gorge: A deep, narrow valley that has steep sides and is usually smaller than a canyon

grassland: Land covered in grasses instead of shrubs and trees; a prairie is a type of grassland.

habitat: Natural home of a plant or animal

historical site: A structure or location where a special event or activity in history took place

landmark: An object or structure that marks a specific location or point of interest; a natural landmark is formed by forces in nature.

landscape: Part of the Earth's surface that can be viewed at one time from one place

national park: An area of land set aside and protected by the government to preserve the special features within it

naturalist: A specialist who studies living things in nature

observation tower: A structure that

allows for a full and clear view of a landscape

paleontology: The science that deals with past living things through the recovery and study of fossils

panoramic: A complete view of a landscape in every direction

permit: A written form of permission to do something, like camp at a special spot or fish in a certain stream

precipitation: All of the forms in which water falls to the ground from the atmosphere, including rain and snow

ranger: A person who is in charge of helping protect and maintain special land, such as a national park

refuge: A place that provides protection for animals, especially endangered ones

sand dune: A mound of sand piled up by the wind

species: A group of plants or animals that share common characteristics

summit: The highest point, like the peak of a mountain

terrain: The surface features of land

topography: On a map, the illustration of features such as heights and depths

wetland: Land that is either covered or soaked by water, such as swamps, for at least part of the year

wildlife: Plants and animals that are found in nature

woodland: Land covered with trees and shrubs

Find Out More

For games and the online Junior Ranger Program visit: **www.nps.gov/webrangers.**

You'll find even more fun with the National Park Service Park Fun Guide: **www.nps.gov/learn/gozone.htm.**

For more national park adventures download "Parks for Play" from the National Park Foundation: **www.nationalparks.org/explore/download-center.**

To learn about park geology and history visit the U.S. Geological Survey: **3dparks.wr.usgs.gov.**

For games and great animal information visit: **kids.nationalgeographic.com.**

To learn more about Buddy Bison and the National Park Trust visit: **www. buddybison.org and www.parktrust.org.**

Index

Index

Credits

*National Geographic gratefully acknowledges the National Park Trust
for use of its mascot, Buddy Bison.*

PUBLISHED BY THE NATIONAL GEOGRAPHIC SOCIETY

John M. Fahey, Jr., *Chairman of the Board and Chief
Executive Officer*
Timothy T. Kelly, *President*
Declan Moore, *Executive Vice President;
President, Publishing*
Melina Gerosa Bellows, *Executive Vice President; Chief
Creative Officer, Books, Kids, and Family*

PREPARED BY THE BOOK DIVISION

Hector Sierra, *Senior Vice President and General Manager*
Nancy Laties Feresten, *Senior Vice President, Editor in Chief,
Children's Books*
Jonathan Halling, *Design Director, Books and
Children's Publishing*
Jay Sumner, *Director of Photography, Children's Publishing*
Jennifer Emmett, *Editorial Director, Children's Books*
Eva Absher-Schantz, *Managing Art Director,
Children's Books*
Carl Mehler, *Director of Maps*
R. Gary Colbert, *Production Director*
Jennifer A. Thornton, *Managing Editor*

STAFF FOR THIS BOOK

Priyanka Lamichhane, *Project Editor*
James Hiscott, Jr., *Art Director*
Lori Epstein, *Senior Illustrations Editor*
Dawn McFadden, *Designer*
Matt W. Chwastyk, Michael McNey, Gregory Ugiansky,
Martin S. Walz, *Map Research and Production*
Grace Hill, *Associate Managing Editor*
Joan Gossett, *Production Editor*
Lewis R. Bassford, *Production Manager*
Susan Borke, *Legal and Business Affairs*
Kate Olesin, *Assistant Editor*
Kathryn Robbins, *Design Production Assistant*
Hillary Moloney, *Illustrations Assistant*

MANUFACTURING AND QUALITY MANAGEMENT

Christopher A. Liedel, *Chief Financial Officer*
Phillip L. Schlosser, *Senior Vice President*
Chris Brown, *Technical Director*
Nicole Elliott, *Manager*
Rachel Faulise, *Manager*
Robert L. Barr, *Manager*

Copyright © 2012 National Geographic Society

 The National Geographic Society is one
of the world's largest nonprofit scientific
and educational organizations. Founded in
1888 to "increase and diffuse geographic
knowledge," the Society works to inspire people to care
about the planet. National Geographic reflects the world
through its magazines, television programs, films, music
and radio, books, DVDs, maps, exhibitions, live events,
school publishing programs, interactive media and
merchandise. *National Geographic* magazine, the Society's
official journal, published in English and 33 local-language
editions, is read by more than 38 million people each
month. The National Geographic Channel reaches 320
million households in 34 languages in 166 countries.
National Geographic Digital Media receives more than 15
million visitors a month. National Geographic has funded
more than 9,400 scientific research, conservation and
exploration projects and supports an education program
promoting geography literacy. For more information, visit
nationalgeographic.com.

For more information, please call 1-800-NGS LINE
(647-5463) or write to the following address:
National Geographic Society
1145 17th Street N.W.
Washington, D.C. 20036-4688 U.S.A.

Visit us online at www.nationalgeographic.com/books

For librarians and teachers: www.ngchildrensbooks.org

More for kids from National Geographic:
kids.nationalgeographic.com

For information about special discounts for bulk
purchases, please contact National Geographic Books
Special Sales: ngspecsales@ngs.org

For rights or permissions inquiries, please contact
National Geographic Books Subsidiary Rights:
ngbookrights@ngs.org

Library of Congress Cataloging-in-Publication Data

National Geographic kids national parks guide U.S.A. : the
most amazing sights, scenes, and cool activities from
coast to coast/National Geographic.
p. cm.
Includes index.
ISBN 978-1-4263-0932-8 (library binding : alk. paper) —
ISBN 978-1-4263-0931-1 (pbk. : alk. paper)
1. National parks and reserves—United States—
Guidebooks—Juvenile literature. 2. United States—
Description and travel—Guidebooks—Juvenile literature.
I. National Geographic Society (U.S.)
E160.N2434 2012
917.3'04—dc23

2011034235

Printed in China
12/RRDS/1

**Neither the publisher nor the author shall be liable
for any bodily harm that may be caused or sustained
as a result of conducting any of the activities
described in this book.**

**Buddy Bison appears 27
times throughout this book.**